A Shell Guide

SOUTH-WEST WALES

Part of Dyfed. The old counties of
Carmarthenshire and Pembrokeshire

A Shell Guide

SOUTH-WEST WALES

Part of Dyfed. The old counties of
Carmarthenshire and Pembrokeshire

by Vyvyan Rees

Faber & Faber 3 Queen Square London

First published in 1963
Second edition published in 1976
First published in Faber Paperbacks in 1982
by Faber and Faber Limited
3 Queen Square London WC1
Printed in Great Britain by
Butler & Tanner Ltd
Frome and London
All rights reserved

Although sponsoring this book, Shell U.K. Ltd would point out that the author is expressing his own views.

British Library Cataloguing in Publication Data

Rees, Vyvyan
    South-west Wales: A Shell guide.—2nd ed.
    1. Wales, South-west—Description and travel—Guide-books
    I. Title
    914.29′4′04857   DA740.S65

ISBN 0–571–04810–2
ISBN 0–571–11820–8 Pbk

Contents

Acknowledgements

This edition enlarges and revises the first one, published in 1963. Since then the two counties have been merged into the new county of Dyfed, which also covers Cardiganshire. I have dealt in greater detail with the changing industrial pattern along the south-eastern coast of Carmarthenshire, with man's encroachment on the uplands, and with the growing significance of agriculture.

I acknowledge with thanks the help given me by the museum curators and librarians of both counties: the officials of county, district and borough councils and of public utilities and commercial undertakings: the National Library of Wales: the R.I.B.A. Library Drawings Collections: the officers of the West Wales Naturalists' Trust, the Pembrokeshire National Parks Committee and Countryside Unit, and the Field Studies Council at Dale and Orielton. Also, too numerous to mention individually, I thank those who have opened their houses to me and the clergy of all denominations who have helped me. My description and details of Picton Castle, near Haverfordwest, are taken by permission of the Editor from articles published by *Country Life* and my old friend Mr H. Lloyd Perkins of St Nicholas has allowed me extensive use of his valuable notes on farming in Pembrokeshire. Finally, I owe a great debt to the General Editor, Mr John Piper, for his encouragement, patience and practical help.

"To any Welsh reader I would say what Michael Drayton in a foreword to his *Polyolbion*, says, speaking of Wales: 'if I have not done her right the want is in my ability not in my love'" (From the introduction to *In Parenthesis*, by David Jones.)

Vyvyan Rees.

Note. Unless otherwise stated none of the houses mentioned in this Guide is open to the public.

Illustrations

Carmarthenshire: Introduction

The largest Welsh county; one's first and last impression, after leaving the high country and forest plantations which fence in so much of it, is of small, always green fields and modest, white-washed farms in a countryside broken by lesser hills and ridges and watered by innumerable rivers and streams. This pattern is reasserting itself in the southern coastal strip, where a second industrial revolution is changing the community life of the county's most populous area.

The Teifi river flowing west into Cardigan Bay forms much of the county's northern boundary. It splits the market towns of Newcastle Emlyn, Llandyssul, Llanybyther and Lampeter between two counties, so establishing close ties with Cardiganshire. Where, at Lampeter, it ceases to form the

northern boundary, that function is assumed by the south-western limb of the Cambrian Range, the spinal cord of mid Wales, above Llandovery and across the fringe of that vast anonymous desert of moorland which lies between the western and the eastern counties of mid Wales. After dropping into the valley, where the A40 highway enters the county, the boundary follows the line of the Carmarthen Vans, an extension of the Brecon Beacons, which merge into the Black Mountains, as far as the Amman valley. Here the Loughor river flowing due south into Carmarthen Bay forms the boundary with Glamorgan and the Swansea valley complex.

The hills overlooking the Teifi valley rarely rise above 1,000 feet, and are cultivated except for stretches of heathland south of Newcastle Emlyn. A feature of them are the lines of laburnum trees, at their best in June, in the roadside hedges. East of Lam-

◁ Garn Goch, **Llangadog**

The Carmarthen Vans (Bannau Sir Gaer) from near **Llanddeusant**

peter, where the altitude rises to 1,500 feet, cultivation virtually ceases except for forestry, and there is splendid walking country off the Mountain Road from Caeo parish over to Llanddewi Brefi. It is accessible enough by car, but soon the silence and solitude envelop all. It is a country of spring water, rushes, acre on acre of seemingly lush grass on which mountain sheep and family groups of mountain ponies graze; no walls, no fences, except perhaps along plantation edges or where, in a hollow, trees give shelter to a lonely farmhouse. The views are immense, the horizons seemingly endless across the world's roof; a smooth, eroded landscape lacking the drama of weather-resistant peaks or lesser outcrops of rocks. So it is, too, on

the savannah-like plateau below the 2,500 feet high sandstone escarpment of the Carmarthen Vans, accessible from the Mountain Road from Trecastle in Brecon to the Tywi valley by way of Llanddeusant.

The high rainfall of the hills, averaging as much as 62 inches a year in the desert above Llandovery, drains either into the Teifi basin, or on to the central plain through valleys often of special beauty and interest; such is the narrow Cych in the north-west corner, green and still, leading to the Teifi; the Cothi joining the Tywi between Llandeilo and Carmarthen, a valley of gorges, forests, and wide stretches near the gold mines at Dolau-

Caeo

cothi; the Bran with immense views down the Tywi valley from the Sugar Loaf ridge on A483 above Llandovery; the Sawdde which meets the Tywi valley at Llangadog, gently winding through Arcadian country below the Black Mountains; and the Cennen and its grimly romantic castle high on a limestone crag.

So, sheltered and watered from the north and east, and open to mild Atlantic air from the south and west, the alluvial Tywi plain, which opens like a horn of plenty at Llandovery, is rich in pasture and maintains the pattern of small farm holdings and fields, so characteristic of the whole of rural Wales. Similarly in the west of the county towards Pembrokeshire and beyond the line where the Tywi, meeting tidal water at Carmarthen, turns due south, the pattern of agriculture is fragmented and essentially pastoral; corn is rarely seen. The inland country, here in the west, is a maze of lanes and abrupt, hidden valleys of great serenity; well watered, too, by the Taf which rises in the Preseli hills in Pembrokeshire to flow south into Carmarthen Bay, and by innumerable smaller streams.

The old industrial area is within a narrow coastal strip between Carmarthen Bay and the Gwendraeth valley, from Kidwelly to the eastern boundary at Glanamman. Two plants, the Trostre Tin Plate Works and the Cynheidre Anthracite Colliery, both near Llanelli, epitomise the second industrial revolution. The first began at the close of the 18th century with the exploitation of the coal seams around Llanelli, which then had a population of 600, and local iron ores. The smelting area is still called Furnace. The finance and drive came from English speculators and ironmasters; iron soon gave way to copper, and copper to steel and to tinplate. By 1914, 90 per cent of British tinplate came from this corner of south Wales. Llanelli earned the name of Tinopolis. Between the two world wars the need to reorganise the industry into fewer and more modern units

pp 14/15 (*above*) Carreg Cennen castle (*below*) The Tywi in flood from Dryslwyn castle (before flood control): Paxton's Tower on the left ▷

became obvious. The second industrial revolution and the economic transformation of the area began in 1946 with the formation of the Steel Company of Wales, integrating the giant steelworks of Port Talbot and the tinplate works of Trostre, and Velindre near Swansea. Trostre started production in 1953 and rapidly adopted the latest tinning techniques. Now Trostre and one steel works, too small to be nationalised, are all that is left of the 40 or so metallurgical units working in Llanelli in 1945.

As with metallurgy, so with coal. Cynheidre and Betws (near Ammanford) collieries, integrated into the National Coal Board, are virtually all that is left of the innumerable mine and drift workings which dotted the anthracite field along the Gwendraeth and Amman valleys. This anthracite field has the only known reserves of high grade anthracite in Britain, and is the only such field in Europe close to tide water. Extensive mining started in the mid-19th century, when new processes made the coal suitable for blast furnaces. There are a few collieries outside the N.C.B. under private licences, which restrict the number of underground workers to 30.

Outside Llanelli, the old industrial area has kept its pattern of village units with a strong community structure still resting on a pre-industrial farming base, and held together by an abiding attachment to Welsh culture, language and Rugby football. As the need for labour drops in the coalfield, the people of the mining villages look to the coastal towns, in our case Llanelli, for work in new factories handling products as diverse as car components, rubber and chemicals. But male unemployment is high as these industries look to female labour, first pressed into service in the wartime munitions factory at Pembrey. So the villages west of Ammanford

◁ **Talley** lakes and **Cenarth** falls

take on a dormitory pattern for Llanelli, as the Amman valley to the east does for Swansea. As none is more than ten miles from the sea, they are well placed as dormitories, on a warm south-facing coast.

The sandy beaches are there, west of Burry Port, the longest stretches in Wales; but they are either so difficult to reach as yet, or so restricted and jealously guarded for purposes other than recreation, that little use can be made of them. It is estimated that 500,000 people live within an hour's drive of Pembrey sands and three times as many within two hours. But desolate acres of a wartime munition factory blot the beach from the coast road. The few who find their way to the sea have plenty of space, despite about two square miles of a Forestry Commission plantation of Corsican Pines, and, at the northern end, a small R.A.F. range. Above all they find peace; there are no amenities, no facilities and therefore no crowds. Local resistance has thwarted a scheme to turn Pembrey into another testing ground for weaponry, and now there is talk of converting 600 acres of an abandoned gunnery range into a park or recreation centre.

So crowds pass by Pembrey sands, either because they do not know they are there or because their wilderness lacks appeal. They hurry westward to Pendine where their maps show a six mile stretch of sand, and where the bathing is safe and amenities abound. Here, however, the Ministry of Defence has for some time found that this stretch of sand is ideal as a firing range, and, while firing is on, the public is barred from all but one third of a mile, which often holds as many as 3,000 cars. Westward again there is a two-mile stretch of sand on Marros beach, but no access by car.

Man's necessities and the discipline which go with them are not confined to the beaches; they encroach more and more on the solitude of the high country and its valley slopes. The thirst for water in the Swansea area has recently led to the creation of Llyn Brianne reservoir on the edge of the desert above Llandovery, impounding the head water of the Tywi. An artificial element is introduced, naturally alien, disturbing contours and folds; the black coil of a scenic route is easier on the suspension than on the eye. The voice of Authority is being heard in the land, injunctions to do this and refrain from that; litter bins, laybys and perhaps in time that most bizarre request of all, "Please do not feed the sheep". Many local people fear that once this wilderness loses its anonymity (there was no Llyn Brianne before the reservoir), and becomes a National Park like Snowdonia or the Beacons, the present tourist trickle will become a flood. It is hard to reconcile a desire for privacy and solitude with that of a vaster public for "scenery", if only seen through the window of a car or motor coach.

Forestry too absorbs more and more of the empty spaces. Plantations are evident below the Vans in the Sawdde valley, and, most pronounced, along and above the Cothi valley, in the Brechfa district. They introduce yet another artificial element. The curlews and lapwings retreat further into the desert, and the hill farmer to a tidy villa on the outskirts of his market town. His epitaph, and that of the way of life which goes with him, is written in the poem *Rhydcymerau* by David Gwenallt Jones (English translation in the *Penguin Book of Welsh Verse*). But forestry provides sorely needed, regular, and satisfying work, more than hill farms do; it helps to build and maintain village communities; its new roads, though closed to motor cars, are welcomed by those who prefer forest trails on foot or pony to open country. The plantations certainly can be sombre, but banks of larch are aflame with colour in autumn. For amenity, clumps of deciduous trees break the monotony of conifers and roadside banks of Lawson's Cupressus screen the dark forest interiors. Some would like it otherwise. The timber—Sitka and Norway Spruce, Firs, Pines and Western Hemlock—has an aver-

Carmarthenshire castles: **Kidwelly, Dryslwyn, Llanstephan** ▷

Taliaris, **Llandeilo**

age life of 50 years and is used mainly for pulping and chipboard. Larch, felled earlier, goes for pitprops; it gives warning of stresses (miners say it talks).

The county roads are good. East to west A40 is scenically dull, and almost unbearably traffic-laden at peak holiday times but it can be avoided as far as Carmarthen, the bottleneck of south Wales, by the Mountain Road from Trecastle in Brecon, which gives the east/west traveller his first close view of moorland, and by roads south of the Tywi. A483, entering the county from further north, is scenically dramatic above the gorge of Bran valley. A most spectacular road, A4069, climbs from the Tywi plain from Llangadog to Brynamman. The Mountain Road from Farmers over the northern

border to Llandewi Brefi climbs into wild country and is not difficult.

Pre-history is evidenced by two dolmens, or remains of burial chambers, one in Llangynog parish, the other in Llanboidy, both associated in their Welsh names, after 3,000 years or so had passed and their purpose and builders long forgotten, with Arthur's legendary hunt of the boar Twrch Trwyth. Bronze Age cairns and barrows (Crug on the Ordnance maps) dot the higher ground. The Iron Age of the Celts is impressively represented by Garn Goch hillfort in Llangadog parish, a place of refuge in times of trouble. The Romans trod more heavily here than had been thought before excavations in Carmarthen revealed the site of a sizeable fort, and similarly in 1972 at Dolaucothi in connection with the gold mines (*see* Caeo). Inscribed stones and relics of the Dark Ages are best represented by the Voteporix stone in Carmarthen Museum.

Norman and Welsh chieftains have left their mark in the great castle of Kidwelly, one of the best and most remote in Wales, and, among others, in the lesser and more romantically sited Llanstephan, Dryslwyn, Carreg Cennen and Dynevor. On the coast from Laugharne to Pendine English is the native tongue, brought by settlers in the 12th century alongside their kin in south Pembrokeshire and the Gower.

The only house so grand as to make the onlooker feel small is Wyatville's Gothic extravagance at Golden Grove, at odds with the gentle, rounded landscape. Cwmgwili, so fine on the hillside over the valley from Bronwydd Arms, has the hall and solar plan of the earliest houses. The 18th century is best represented by Taliaris in Llandeilo parish, and, later, by Plas in Llanstephan. Many others are in ruin, empty or a heap of stones; Middleton Hall, Edwinsford, Iscoed, Llysnewydd (for locations *see* index and for John Nash *see* Carmarthen).

Other than Llanelli, the towns, essentially market, lie along the Tywi plain—Llandovery, Llandeilo, Carmarthen. They show the Welsh characteristics of small, self assertiveness, in architecture of the 18th and early 19th centuries. Squares and terraces have an individuality and character hitherto little recognised since the architectural merit of particular buildings is not remarkable. But in combination they have a pleasant complexion and one personal to Wales. Often sited on a river, they may have an ancient bridge and a Norman mound to add character and romance; houses climbing above river banks carry the eye upward to new perspectives. Laugharne and Llanstephan on the coast have the same architectural qualities, but, cut off from the main traffic stream, they are more aloof and well content to remain so. Kidwelly sleeps on in its castle's shade. Llanelli streets have a special quality; mostly early 19th century, the rows of houses are planned with a conviction in lay out and an eye for detail (Classical, Gothic, Tudor). They recall the early paintings of Giorgio de Chirico. There are good contemporary buildings at Trinity College, Carmarthen. As to churches there is nothing very exciting in the larger towns; too many of the county churches were so neglected in the 18th and 19th centuries that complete rebuilding was the only answer, and, to-day, rural depopulation has left many of those sadly in need of repair. The Priory church at Kidwelly is an exception. There is striking modern stained glass by Lawrence Lee at Betws outside Ammanford, John Petts at Llandovery, John Hayward at Llanllawdog and Patrick Feeny in the Roman Catholic church at Llanelli and earlyish Victorian glass by J. Bell, Bristol, at Carmarthen and Llanboidy. Chapel architecture is well represented in its original 18th- and 19th-century form, and in Llanelli, Llandeilo and Carmarthen there are interesting examples of late Victorian and early 20th-century pastiches of the classical, the work of such local architects as George Morgan of Carmarthen and David Jenkins of Llandeilo.

Some knowledge of early church history in Wales will help to a fuller appreciation of church and chapel. At the Reformation, the large domains of the church, where local religious houses had ensured a high standard of agriculture and had embellished their places of worship, were handed over often to alien landlords, keener on their rent roll than on sound farming and upkeep. Barely had the reformed church begun to establish itself in the trust of the Welsh people when the Puritans came to power. Royalism and the old faith were dying hard in Wales, and special commissioners were appointed to speed the process. Sir John Lloyd in his History of Carmarthenshire says of the Puritans "They succeeded in ejecting the clergy, appropriating the emoluments, demolishing works of art, destroying organs, burning prayer books but they failed to build a single vestry".

Llandeilo and (*below*) Llandovery ▷

Stained glass windows were destroyed as Popish. In the 18th century Nonconformity was a revolt from within the church against absentee rectors enjoying rich stipends, but leaving the care to ill-paid curates, and against neglect in high places. Clergy defied their masters by preaching to their people in their own tongue. Suspended from their office, they left the church in despair, to carry on their work as independent preachers. They revived religion in Wales and turned mainly to Calvinism. They have been the means of preserving the Welsh language. Wisely under the 1919 Disestablishment Act, the established church in Wales was freed from state control and dependence on West-minster or Canterbury. It has its own Constitution and Governing Body.

To recapture lost time look for the villages in the foothills, out of the stream of traffic, Myddfai, Caeo, Llansadwrn, Llansawel, Brechfa, Abergorlech, Llanfynydd, to name some. Unlike the general run of straggling Welsh villages, these are small contained units, grouped around their church. Under Midland influence their pubs may have their cocktail bars, exposed rafters and copper coaching horns, but outside the feeling is one of indifference to time. The milk lorry clatters through, the school bus picks up or drops its load, a dog barks at the sight of a stranger. The church is locked, the parson may be out with Meals on Wheels, but the key if it is not hanging in the porch is probably at the village shop.

◁ Pattern and texture:
Llansawel and (*below*) **Llandovery**

Carmarthenshire: Gazetteer

The number in brackets refers to the square on the map at the end of the book where the place is to be found.

ABERGORLECH. *See* LLANY-BYTHER.

ABERGWILI [14] The *Bishop of St David's Palace*, which replaces one destroyed by fire, lies in the meadowland where the Tywi and Gwili rivers meet. It is now being rebuilt to fit modern domestic needs. Adjacent, the church, designed by C. C. Nelson and altered in 1889 by E. Christian, is spacious but darkened by a heavily timbered roof and 19c stained glass, one window to the memory of Captain Phillips R.N. last survivor of the Battle of the Nile. *Cwmgwili*, the principal house of the district, is a large, white two-storeyed house with dormer windows, clearly visible from the Bronwydd Arms to Cynwyl Elfed road. It has its origins in the early hall and solar type dwelling. It was altered in the 17c and has a staircase of about 1640 and panelling. On the eastern boundary of the parish beyond Felin Wen and above A40 there is another church at *Llanfihangel uwch Gwili*, in a very narrow lane. The shortened tower is probably 16c, and the small nave and chancel are very decorous and modern.

ABERNANT [13] A curious feature of this parish is that the dead were brought to the 3-acre churchyard for burial from places far beyond the parish boundary, implying that the site had some special and ancient significance. The village in its valley setting is insignificant and the 13c church was almost entirely rebuilt in the 19c. *Talog*, a hamlet to the north, lies in a green and quiet valley.

AMMANFORD [15] Has a clean and lively look. It is the main shopping centre for the Amman valley, and has none of the usual features of a mining town. The parish church (1915) on the hillside was designed by David Jenkins of Llandeilo; plain Gothic inside; you can sense the Nonconformist in Jenkins by the meagre chancel and sanctuary. The *Welsh Church* in Wind Street is built of boulders from the Amman valley. The workmanship is better than the effect.

BETWS [15] A mining village with an active anthracite mine, over the river from Ammanford. The small church was rebuilt, except for the Early English south door, by R. K. Penson in 1872. East window (1960) by Lawrence Lee, who designed some of the windows for Coventry Cathedral. The design, inspired by Williams, Pantycelyn's, hymn *Guide me O Thou Great Jehovah* conveys in Lee's own words "the struggle, failure and prayer of the Chris-tian, with the answering Christ as Strong Deliverer".

BRECHFA. *See* LLANEGWAD.

BRYNAMMAN. *See* CWMAM-MAN.

BURRY PORT [17] The industrial tendency out of Llanelli is now eastward towards Swansea, so that the old working area towards Pembrey has stagnated, and the lower hillside slopes are becoming more and more residential. From the important *Carmarthen Bay Power Station* pylons and cables extend across the south of the county.

CAEO or CYNWYL GAEO [12] The Ogofau gold workings are off the A482 in National Trust land near Dolaucothi. The Celts had found gold here, and the Romans lost no time in exploiting the veins by open cast and gallery working. They created the most advanced mining site technologically of its time in Europe. They were aided by adequate water from the rivers Cothi and Annell, which they brought down by a seven-mile-long aequeduct, channelled along the hillsides. The water was stored in tanks cut into the rocks, from which it was sluiced to remove top soil, wash the crushed ore and drive simple machinery. At its peak the workings yielded about one

hundredweight of gold a week which was taken to Lyons and possibly Rome for minting. Recent excavations in the grounds of the *Dolaucothi Arms Hotel* have revealed the foundations of a fortified base, workshops, granary, and evidence of glass as well as gold smelting. Nothing much is known of the mines' history after about the middle of the 2c when the Romans left the site until about 1870, when an Australian named Mitchell reopened many of the Roman galleries. Work continued under different ownerships until 1939. Amateurs should explore the open galleries with caution. It is interesting to compare the earliest chisel and wedge cut walls with later mechanical and explosive methods. There is no trace of the Roman bath house noted on O.S. maps, but the importance of the site must have meant a large settlement and much remains to be found.

Dolaucothi Hall, for which Nash designed a new front, has been demolished but some splendid trees remain in the park, and there is an estate feeling about the diamond latticed windows of the houses and lodges around. Frances Hodgkins, the New Zealand artist, painted a series of farm scenes during the last war from the Dolaucothi Arms Hotel. The colour-washed cottages of *Caeo* village are grouped on a hillside around the massive 13c towered church, much restored in the 1890s. The vault of the Johnes family of Dolaucothi is against

Roman gold mines at Dolaucothi, **Caeo**

the west wall, enclosed in ornate wrought-iron railings.

To the north, *Farmers*, on the Roman Sarn Helen road, is a pretty hamlet of the Drovers Arms and blue and white cottages. Northward beyond Farmers, the *Mountain Road* to Llanddewi Brefi crosses desolate open country to climb the mountain side, the upper slopes of which are covered by the *Esgair Goch* forestry plantations which contrast with the rough pasture and rush grown land to the east, the swampy source of the Cothi and other small streams.

At *Crug y bar*, off B4302 to Llansawel, there is a pretty, Congregational chapel in delicate shades of white, grey and pink, mainly 1765 and 1837. A plaintive hymn tune sung at funerals takes its name from this hamlet.

Lewis Glyn Cothi (1447–1486), poet very much in the bardic tradition, also sang of nature as Dafydd ap Gwilym had done, a hundred years earlier. He is now best known for his lament for his small son, Siôn.

CARMARTHEN [13] Thriving market town, in Welsh *Caerfyrddin or Merlin's Camp*. Its situation on and above the tidal Tywi ensured its importance as a trading centre far back in the Middle Ages, and, to-day, scenically, lifts it out of the ordinary. Attempts to divert through traffic from its narrow medieval streets are only moderately successful. A dual carriageway west of the town on A40 gives short promise of better things. There is modern development at Johnstown on the Llanstephan road, a modern school, some light industry, and Unigate's expanding milk processing plant, to which a cheese unit with a manufacturing capacity of over 100,000 gallons a day has been added.

Early architecture is Celtic in its disdain for civic embellishment. The 1770 *Guildhall* in the centre of the town is homespun Palladian, and the front of the slightly earlier *Furness House*, opposite St Peter's Church, is square, with well-proportioned windows. *King Street* has one or two good Georgian doorways; there is a short row of Georgian houses, one of them the *County Museum* (worth a visit), in *Quay Street*. The *Parade* is lined on one side by a variety of architectural styles from the beginning of the 19c onwards and from it there is a fine view, with railway yards in the foreground, of the Tywi valley and the grassy and tree-decked knolls which rise like a Patinir landscape so curiously and abruptly from the valley bed. The *County Hall*, partly on the site of the vanishing Norman castle, was begun in 1939 and finished in 1955 to the design of Sir Percy Thomas of Cardiff. The high, steeply pitched roof and the cone-topped angle turrets in the early French Renaissance style introduce a different architectural style. The green-grey roof slates are of Tyrch stone from the Preseli hills in Pembrokeshire and match the Pennant stone of the walls.

Church and chapel architecture follows the usual Welsh county town pattern. The central parish church, plain and Perpendicular in style, has the grand tomb of Sir Rhys ap Thomas and his wife. Sir Rhys led the Welsh contingent with Henry Tudor to Bosworth and on to London. He retired to Carew in Pembrokeshire and died in the Franciscan Friary in Carmarthen in 1525. 1864 window in east wall of south aisle by J. Bell of Bristol. Two suburban churches on the western outskirts, both by R. K. Penson, are more stylish inside than outside. The 1850-ish *Roman Catholic Church*, also in this area, glows inside with light and colour. The most interesting chapel, architecturally, is the *1872 English Baptist* in Lammas Street. Here the local architect and builder, George Morgan of King Street, has indulged to the full his liking for the tall Corinthian column. John Nash came from London in 1784 to practise in Carmarthen, probably, although he would not admit it, licking the wounds of insolvency, and stayed for twelve years or so. Here he engaged as draughtsman, A. C. Pugin, a refugee from France. He lived in the very ordinary house at right-angles to Francis Terrace (and now the caretaker's house for Pentre Porth school), and all his known work in the county has either been replaced (as the memorial to General Sir Thomas Picton, killed at Waterloo, and the roof of St Peter's church) or has been demolished. The *Queen Elizabeth Grammar School*, on the hill above the town, has been since 1576 the most notable centre of education in this district. To the west of the town, the *Trinity Training College*, whose large 19c buildings by Henry Clutton (1848), replace the original

ones, has had later additions, including works by Sealy and Paget of the 1920s, and the Architects Co-Partnership— the most distinguished contemporary architecture in the county.

CASTELL DWYRAN. *See* LLANDISSILIO EAST.

CENARTH [10] In summertime crowds flock to the village centre, where the counties of Carmarthen, Pembroke and Cardigan meet, to see the Teifi cascading over rocky ledges into pools above an old stone bridge and, perhaps, to see a salmon leaping the falls. In early spring sheep are washed in the pools before shearing, and coracle men are on hand to prevent any from being swept downstream. Of the coracle fishermen only two are left now (1973) and their licences to take salmon and sewin die with them. Stone and colour-wash cottages, with a church to crown them, adorn the village on the northern edge of a large mountain and valley parish with an average of one person to twenty acres. The church, designed by the Cheltenham architects, Middleton and Goodman, is a simple nave and chancel building, apsidal, light and lofty. Rose window in the west wall and pleasantly "period" late 19c stained glass. The round font basin is decorated with rudely carved masks, 13c. The main road to Newcastle Emlyn follows the river but there is a secondary

Carmarthen
left English Baptist Chapel
right Picton memorial

Cenarth bridge

road leading off, opposite the church. It has views over Cardiganshire and passes the entrance to *Gelli Dywyll*, an early 18c house, now empty but with solid, occupied, and earlier farm buildings adjacent.

CILYCWM [12] Picturesque village street with cobbled edges and, behind the inn, a 15c church fortunate in its 1904 restoration by W. D. Caröe. It has the familiar plain west tower, and south aisle. The Perpendicular east window of three small lights glows with late 19c stained glass (T. Baillie; The

Last Supper). In the south aisle below a barrel roof, a family box pew; frescoes including the Royal Arms on the east wall, Creed and Commandments partially obscured by memorials, and, on the west wall, a skeleton holding a spear, probably 15c. Enormous yew tree outside.

Northward, at *Tywi Bridge Inn*, cottages and a tiny Baptist hillside chapel are white squares on the green background. Beyond, the valley becomes a defile and the high hills are lost to side view in a tangle of beech, scrub oak, and

heather on their lower slopes. There is a "picturesque" waterfall at *Nant Melyn* and, below it, white *Bwlch y rhiw* Baptist chapel (1717/1906) among meadowsweet and rushes. Here the road deserts the Tywi for the Cothi and boomerangs back into cultivated land in Caeo parish. The whole is an unforgettable journey.

CILYMAENLLWYD [6] A large rolling Pembrokeshire border parish, taking in part of *Llanglydwen* village, including its church, which lies above the valley. To reach the church you

◁ **Cenarth** mill

pass under a Gothic castellated archway, built around two gatepost boulders, marking the entrance to *Dolwilym*, an 18c house with 19c refacing. The church, partially restored on old foundations in the last century, is well lit through clear glass windows in the nave. 18c monuments, stone tiles, and at the entrance to the churchyard a very early stone, itself roughly the shape of a cross, carries carved in relief a plain cross, in a circle.

Two miles east of Llanglydwen, at the entrance to Froganol farm, with a fine aspect over the Taf valley, the 1770 church Eglwys Fair a Churig is abandoned in a brambled churchyard. At the hamlet of *Efailwen* the *Rebecca riots* started in 1839 with the destruction of the tollgate and burning of the tollhouse. The last peasant revolt in Britain, it was an uprising, at a time of agricultural depression, against the levying of tolls, particularly on the movement of lime and other necessities from the coast. The rioters were dressed as women, an allusion to Isaac's bride, (*see* Genesis 24.60) and the leader and his followers were known as Rebecca and her daughters. Troops sent to quell the disturbances were easily outwitted in the maze of lanes, but, as regulations were relaxed, and agriculture became more profitable, the movement gradually petered out. David Williams' book *The Rebecca Riots* (University of Wales Press 1955) tells the story well.

CONWIL ELVET *see* CYNWYL ELFED

CWMAMMAN [15] Takes in *Brynamman* and *Glanamman*, an endless road of terraced houses, in the valley south of the Black Mountains, once dependent on anthracite mining. Now there is some private open-cast working employing few men. The factories and industries of Swansea today offer alternative employment. Imposing chapel in Glanamman Square, and a simple church in Brynamman by Ebbels, twice restored since 1842.

CYNWYL ELFED or CONWIL ELVET. [13] Village on a hill with a partly 14c church. Tinted glass windows throughout in geometric and leaf patterns darken the Victorian interior. The east window symbolises the Crucifixion; Head, Heart and Hands of Christ are embraced in an abstract design within the framework of the Cross. Northward B4333, a fast, moorland road with views over Cardiganshire carries little traffic.

EGLWYS CYMYN [6] A large, thinly populated parish, stretching from Carmarthen Bay at Marros inland to the outskirts of Whitland. The parish church on the Pendine/Red Roses road is dedicated to St Margaret, Queen of Scotland, whose descendant Guy de Brian partly rebuilt it in the 14c (see also Llandowror). It is a simple, primitive building with vaulted roof and white plastered walls, round-headed chancel arch, oak pews, stone floor, and benches in the porch, and a Benefaction Board. A chained Bible of the first edition to be printed in Welsh by Peter

Williams (a curate here), a Latin/Ogam inscribed stone in an oak coffer and a pilgrim bottle are treasures. There is a lonely, neglected 13c towered church, high in the hills at *Cyffig*, south of Whitland, and, at *Marros*, west of Pendine, an 1844 church with a top heavy tower, also of the 13c. Outside the church, on open ground a 1914–1918 War Memorial is a trilithon: two upright stone slabs with a capstone. A lane leads towards Marros beach, but gates are locked against motor traffic, and the beach, morose and bordered by small hedged fields below the cliffs, is barely accessible. *Marros Mountain* is an expanse of moorland with some forestry. Very prosperous farming country.

EGLWYS FAIR A CHURIG. *See* CILYMAENLLWYD.

FERRYSIDE. *See* ST ISHMAELS.

HENLLAN AMGOED. *See* HENLLANFALLTEG.

HENLLANFALLTEG [6] Includes Llanfallteg East and Henllan Amgoed, in deeply rural settings and lost in the lanes north of Whitland. Big Victorian house, *Tegfynydd*, in conifer and other trees at Llanfallteg. At Henllan Amgoed a lonely, sad Victorian church, and a massive Congregational chapel, one of the county's oldest, now dully modernised, overlooking a large burial ground.

KIDWELLY [16] Took pride in its borough status arising from its Norman foundation, but the silting of the Gwendraeth Fach

Cynwyl Elfed: The five wounds in the Victorian east window ▷

estuary in the 17c caused the decline of this once flourishing seaport until it is now a big village. There is some ugly modern development, but the castle, one of the best in Wales, whose buildings range in date from about 1275 (towers and curtain walls) to the 16c (outer hall), rears above all. Now in the hands of the Department of the Environment, although the property of the Earl of Cawdor. Some of the towers are complete to their turrets and there is Early English work in the chapel. The medieval settlement is in two parts; on the river's west bank, the castle and the walled town, and on the other side, connected by a medieval bridge of two arches the new town and the 13c Benedictine Priory church of St Mary, the most distinguished in the county. The southern, 14c, gatehouse of the old town still stands. The dominant feature of the church is a steeple-capped tower. Inside, light floods in through clear glass, and stained glass is almost entirely confined to the east and west windows, the latter by Celtic Studios. The 1762 organ is by Thomas Warne. There are traces of early iron foundries in the built up part of the borough and seaward the salt marshes once supported large flocks of sheep. The works with the tall chimneys near the marshes, which made silica bricks, are now closed.

LAUGHARNE [13] Stephen Lewis in his 1833 *Topographical Dictionary of Wales* says: "The appearance of the town, which is considered one of the cleanest and best built in South Wales, embosomed in an amphitheatre

Narrow gauge trolleys at the ruined tinplate works, **Kidwelly**

of verdant hills and ornamented with the venerable remains of its ancient castle, is truly romantic." It is still as he describes it. It once traded with ports on the western shores of Europe, but it had a bad reputation for harbouring Bristol Channel pirates, and, by the time Stephen Lewis wrote, it had become almost entirely agricultural and a retreat for half-pay pensioners. Its charter is 14c and, alienated traditionally from the neighbouring Welsh, it preserved its Norman forms of civil administration, Port reeves, Court Leet and Court Baron, in this "soft kangaroo pocket of the salt, sad

West". It has some excellent houses and a general air of calm assurance. The Norman castle was largely rebuilt by Sir John Perrott (see Carew in Pembrokeshire). It is not generally open to the public. *Castle House* and other houses are Georgian. The church, at the northern entrance, is mainly 15c and sombre. Late 19c stained glass in all windows, high arches to chancel and transepts, and scraped walls heavy with memorial tablets. The grave of Dylan Thomas, marked by a plain white wooden cross, is in the southern extension of the churchyard, out of the shade of the yew trees. His boat-house home has been bought by a trust set up in Wales and will become a museum.

LLANARTHNEY [14] The church, alongside the valley road to Carmarthen was partially rebuilt in 1682, completely rebuilt except for the two lower stages of the 13c tower in 1826 when a south aisle was removed and its present conventicle look acquired, and slightly restored in 1877 when the windows and furniture were renewed. Features are Munich-type stained glass in east window and stone flagged floor. The incised stone in the porch, inscribed in Norman French and Latin is probably 12c. Two chapels; a grey stone one in the village, and another, a pretty Gothic one, across a field from the road towards Middleton Hall. *Middleton Hall*, a fine classical building, designed by S. P. Cockerell in the 1790s for the local magnate Sir William Paxton, was burnt out in 1931, and later razed. But Cockerell's

Paxton's tower, **Llanarthney**

work is still to be seen in the stables and possibly the laundry, now converted into cottages. Later C. R. Cockerell designed the Gothic Paxton's Tower, built to honour Lord Nelson on the highest point of a ridge overlooking the Tywi valley, and conspicuous for miles. It is triangular in plan, with a rounded tower at each angle and high arched openings. Originally it had in its second storey an octagonal banqueting room. A finely coloured portrait of Nelson, apparently on glass which hung here is to be seen in Carmarthen Museum. The tower was given to the nation by the Earl of Cawdor in 1965, and well restored by the Historic Buildings Council through public subscription in 1967. It is now National Trust property.

In the south of the parish there is great enthusiasm for Rugby football and many national heroes live in and around the mining villages from Drefach to Gorslas.

LLANBOIDY [6] A grouped village in the English style and an appendage to Maesgwynne (Powell family) once the principal house. The pub is the *Maesgwynne Arms*, and the village hall was built, as a market hall, from the proceeds of a bet on a horse named Hermit by one of the Powells. The church, in the centre, has in the short south transept an 1849 two light window by J. Bell, Bristol. The church bell is now outside in the churchyard, head high under a wooden cover like a well head. Also in the churchyard, beyond the east end, an 1891 monument by Goscombe John R.A. of a female figure in grief, over the Powell vault. *Maesgwynne*, built in 1684, with a later portico, has lost a wing and has a good arrangement of windows on the east elevation. Till recently a farmhouse, it has changed hands and will probably be put into repair. It has a parkland view and once had a pheasantry and private racecourse. The north-east corner of the parish takes in part of *Llan-glydwen* up to the railway track, the pub and the Pretoria stores. The county's best dolmen, *Gwal y Filiast*, (*Greyhounds' Lair*) is in Forestry Commission woodland east of the railway track. Four thin uprights about three feet out of the ground support an enormous capstone. It can be reached along the railway track, and up through the woods to the east.

LLANDDAROG [14] Partly by-passed by the busy A48 road. Thatched inn and a Surrey style spire to the 1860 church by R. K. Penson.

LLANDAWKE. *See* LLAN-DOWROR.

LLANDDEUSANT [15] The *Mountain Road* from Trecastle in Brecon crosses moorland as far as Cross Inn. Thence a hazard-ous lane runs due south to the church, old rectory and youth hostel, all there is of a village in this large parish which rises from the Tywi valley to the peak of the Carmarthen Vans. The church, pleasantly weathered outside but dull in-side, has bellcote, 14c bits, plastered barrel roof, and an arcade of four arches to the south aisle. An indifferent road and track runs from the church to the northern foot of the sand-stone escarpment of Bannau Sir Gaer, scored as though with tri-bal marks, and to Llyn y fan fach, a natural tarn and the main source of water for the rural districts of Llandeilo and Llanelli. Shallow at the outflow end, its greatest depth is esti-mated at 80 feet. It is fed through a stone channel over a

mile long by surface water, and by a spring within the lake. The average daily output is close on 2,000,000 gallons. The walk from the attractively screened caretaker's lodge is not so arduous as it appears. The more energetic will find it rewarding because there are immense backward views, closer views of boulders and family groups of ponies, and always the sound of running water. Three hundred eels were netted when the lake was partly drained for dam-ming. There is a folk legend associated with this lake about a young farmer who sees a beautiful fairy rowing in a gol-den boat with silver oars. He falls in love with her and mar-ries her. Then by accident he makes three mistakes her father had warned him against, and she disappears into the lake with the fairy cattle she had brought with her. Later she meets her three sons and gives them medical prescriptions, tel-ling them to relieve the world's pain and misery. This legend is connected with the physicians of Myddfai (*see* Myddfai).

LLANDEILO [15] Driving west along A40, you skirt the town and get an impression of a Welsh market town with a thriving trade in machinery. But if you step aside you will find a pleasant parade walk overlooking the Tywi river, and, bordered by early Vic-torian houses, interesting side streets, late 19c and early 20c stone-faced and Gothic chapel architecture, and a fine bridge on the main road to Swansea, with meadowland and gardens at the water's edge. This road bisects the churchyard, in

which tall trees bring shade and contrast into the town centre. The church, rebuilt except for the 13c tower—its best feature—by Sir Gilbert Scott in 1850, lacks character, although there is some colour in the stained glass of the 1914–18 war memorial east window. Celtic cross head, probably 10c, lies on the floor of the north aisle. A large new comprehensive school, designed by the County Architect, has been built in the grounds of Tregeyb at Ffair-fach. *Tregeyb* is a large ugly Vic-torian house, once a Roman Catholic school.

The rural parish, large and rich in natural and man-made beauty, is divided from east to west by the Tywi. On the south it extends over the moorland of the Black Mountains to the Amman valley. A good secon-dary road from *Ffairfach* climbs to the 700-foot contour and down into the Cennen valley at *Trapp* which has a good bridge, a cross-roads maze, and a pretty grey-washed inn, the *Cennen Arms*. Hereabouts you get re-markable views of fairy-like *Carreg Cennen Castle* perched on a limestone precipice overlook-ing the valley, 300 feet below. It is reached by a gradual slope on its east side from a large new car park, with amenities, on the edge of a farmyard. The build-ing is late 13 or early 14c, and is almost certainly on the site of an earlier castle, associated, like neighbouring Dryslwyn and Dynevor, with the Welsh princes of the Lords Rhys, who won back their independence from the Normans. It was taken by the English under Edward I, and what remains now is largely the rebuilding which followed.

Llyn y fan fach (**Llanddeusant**) after snow ▷

The Welsh held it for the Lancastrians in the Wars of the Roses, and on its surrender, partial demolition made it useless as a fortress. After passing to the Cawdor family it was finally placed under the care of what is now the Department of the Environment. It is well worth a visit as it contains within a small compass almost all the main ingredients of a larger castle. South across the Cennen valley *Cwrt Bryn y Beirdd* is a massive

◁ Country near **Llandeilo**

farmhouse of the 16c, with corbels and pointed arch. Across more fields, some ten minutes walk away, the headwaters of the *Loughor river* cascade from a hillside cave, now fenced in.

North of the Tywi line and towards Llandovery a secondary road branches left at *Cwm Ifor* (pale stone-coloured pebble-dash Baptist chapel, 1789–1836–1864; and plain late 19c church with copies of Murillo paintings at *Manordeilo*) and soon rejoins A40. It is worth taking for the alternate views of the Black Mountain to

the south and the hills above the vale of Talley to the north. You pass cupola-topped Hermon Congregational chapel and aisled vestry (1812–1848–1868), in pinkish pebble-dash and with buff eaves. Among the country and farmhouses of the district, *Taliaris*, off the Lampeter Road, is notable. Built in 1638, it has its original Jacobean staircase and a richly-modelled plaster ceiling bearing the arms of the Gwynne family; also fine panelling on all floors. It was remodelled and refronted about 1780, and a

Carreg Cennen Castle (**Llandeilo**)

block with Venetian windows projects from the north side of the west wing. There is an octagonal cockpit in front of it. The house is open to the public by appointment from Whitsun to October.

LLANDEILO ABERCYWYN. *See* LLANGYNOG.

LLANDISSILIO EAST [6] A valley opens up at *Rhydwilym* where there is a tall slate-hung and stone chapel (Baptist 1761) with a presence. It was the mother chapel of the sect as far back as the 17c for a large area extending into north Pembrokeshire and Cardigan. In 1701 some 20 members of the sect sailed for America in the *John and Mary* from Milford, and settled in Delaware. To-day the ceremony of adult baptism by immersion in the Cleddau, opposite the chapel, is followed by another ceremony, similar to that of confirmation. The parish church is over the border in Pembrokeshire, but at the farm gates of *Castell Dwyran* a tiny bellcote church has one service a year. Rebuilt in 1870, and enlarged then by miniature low-arched transepts, its stone floors and pointed lattice windows with clear glass give it character. The doorway is probably 13c. No doubt an ancient site, as the Latin-inscribed *Voteporix* stone, now in Carmarthen museum, came from here.

LLANDOVERY [12] Gateway to the Tywi valley, slighted by 18 and 19c tourists, and now a traffic bottleneck on A40. In the centre, the twice-weekly cattle markets add to the holiday season confusion below the ruins of the Norman castle on its grassy slope, to the interest of those not directly involved. The town has an almost uniformly grey look; stucco and rough casting hide the antiquity of houses, shops, and inns. Trim bungalows and new villas line the main roads which radiate from the centre. For centuries, cattle, pigs and geese were assembled here to be driven over the drovers' trails via Llandulas, south of Llanwrtyd Wells and Rhydyspence on the Hereford border into England. The *Bank of the Black Ox* founded in 1799 by David Jones helped this trade. Its business and pleasantly modernised late Georgian house were taken over by Lloyds Bank in 1909. The drovers acted as bankers; if a man owed a bill in London he would give the money to a drover who banked it at home and paid the bill out of the proceeds of his cattle sales in the London market. Many of the drovers settled in England, and substantial farmers now in the Midlands and Southern Counties can trace their beginnings to the uplands of Wales.

Llandovery College was built in 1848 (architect G. E. Gingell of Bristol), on straightforward Gothic lines. In the chapel there is a crucifixion painting by Graham Sutherland, presented by an old boy, Dr H. J. Powell, and in the hall a St Peter by Guercino, presented by Sir John Llewellyn. Another benefactor, at its foundation, was the famous book collector, Thomas Phillips, one-time Navy Surgeon and inspector of Botany Bay hospitals. He left the college £11,000 in his will and 7,000 books.

There are two churches, Llanfair just off A483, and St Dingad's on the Llangadog road. *Llanfair*, built on a Roman site, has a late 13c tower at the west end with late 15c parapets with gargoyles. Inside, the church, a single-chambered building with 12c features, was restored in 1913 by W. D. CarÖe. Recesses, archways, windows and openings of different periods will delight the pure antiquarian and the most coherent feature is the fine tie beam roof over the nave. There are two hatchments, very showy, of the Gwynne family. The walls are pleasantly plastered, and the stained glass is worth seeing, covering styles from the late Victorian 1870ish window in the south wall of the nave, through Walter Tower's conventional east window depicting Williams Pantycelyn, and Vicar Prichard, and his two windows in the north wall of the chancel all 1920–1930, to three recent windows by John Petts. One is a single light in the west wall, an abstract, geometrical pattern of yellow, orange, pink and mauve, effectively enhancing the glow of the western sun; another is a double light window in the chancel in memory of a soldier missing at Dunkirk, depicting St George dismounted and the dragon bearing the swastika emblem; the third, donated by John Petts, in a lancet slit window almost at ground level in the chancel has, simply, the vertical letters CAR.DI (the Welsh for *Love Thou*), each letter in a square and outlined in black against a background of shades of orange.

A pathway of stone flags,

bordered by cobbles, leads to St *Dingad's*, restored in 1906, also by W. D. Caröe. Apart from the tower and walls it is all his. It has a wealth of Munich glass and modern glass by Leonard Walker. The floor is stone-flagged; pews are stained a greyish green and a cathedral-type Gothic font has unsuitably been built around its simple predecessor. The 1886 *English*

Methodist chapel in High Street (architect J. H. Phillips,) in local and Bath stone comme-morates the famous local hymn writer, W. Williams, Panty-celyn (1717–91). Unusual feature for nonconformist cha-pel is the free-standing pulpit in Caen stone. Three other cha-pels in nearby Queen Street, modestly elegant *Ebenezer* (Baptist 1844, enlarged 1905) in

cream and white with delicate barge-board, cupola-crowned *Salem* (Congregational 1797, rebuilt 1829), stone colour with white window surrounds, and *Tabernacle* (Welsh Methodist 1836), grey with white win-dows, should be seen. One of Llandovery's vicars was Rees Prichard, who died in 1644, the author of *Cannwydd y Cymry* (*the Welshman's Candle*), a book

Llandovery

of simple religious homilies in Welsh. Pant y Celyn, W. Williams' home, is about three miles west of Llandovery.

The bridge over the Twyi west of the town was built about 1790; the architect was Thomas Edwards. What a pity that its outline from upstream should be obscured by an unsightly modern footbridge of tubular steel, braced overhead with flat arches of similar material. Thomas' father, William, built in 1773 the bridge at Dolau Hirion, a mile or so north of the town. It has a span of 84 feet and pierced haunches to relieve flood-water and is a replica of his better-known bridge at Pontypridd.

LLANDOWROR [13] A main road village dominated by the high-towered church. The nave and chancel were rebuilt in the 1860s. Stained glass in east window by A. J. Dix, London, 1904. In the chancel is the tomb of Griffith Jones, rector from 1716 to 1761. He pioneered the county's 18c religious revival. He trained teachers who were then sent to parishes to teach young and old to read the Bible in Welsh. Westward, the main road to south Pembrokeshire winds through meadows and steep banks of conifers. On the seaward side, in the church parish of *Llansadurnen*, the cultivated East Marsh is protected from the sea by a line of dunes and an artificial bank. On its eastern face is the famous *Coygan cave*, in which bones of rhinoceros, hyena, mammoth

Llandovery

and other animals long extinct in Britain have been found. The cliff is now extensively quarried. The church on higher ground to the north was simply rebuilt in 1859. It has views across the marshes to the Gower peninsula.

There is a charming, primitive little 13c church at *Llandawke*. It lies in a hollow with Georgian Llandawke Manor and farm buildings in the background. The setting is delightful. The church has a stone-flagged floor, cream walls, subject to damp, and clear glass except for two coloured panes in the east window. The broken effigy of a female figure in simple and flowing robe, is ascribed in a notice to Margaret Marlos, daughter of the brother-in-law of Guy de Brian (see Eglwys Cymyn). It was found in the churchyard. Also a Latin/Ogam inscribed stone. The low church tower rises barely three feet above the nave roof. (For Ogam stones see footnote to Introduction to Pembrokeshire.)

LLANDYBIE [14] Has not lost its village character and is full of charm and friendliness. Nothing elegant architecturally, but considerable antiquity in some of the houses. The principal house in the village, *Plas*, has been demolished. The church, clumsily enlarged in the 14c, has a fine medieval timber barrel roof, some good 17 and 18c tablets, a hatchment of the Vaughans of Derwydd and an 1814 iron casting of the Royal Arms. The limestone kilns on the Llandeilo road were designed by R. K. Penson, the church architect, in the 1850s,

and the arches reflect his love of the soaring Gothic. He lived for a time at Cefncethin close by, and was partly responsible for the larger-scale exploitation of the quarries under Lime Firms Ltd, in place of the smaller quarrying on a family holding basis. *Derwydd*, one of the houses of the Tudor Sir Rhys ap Thomas, has never passed out of the possession of his descendants. It has fine stone and plaster 1644 mantelpieces and earlier panelling. *Glynhir*, on high ground east of the village, Jacobean with an indifferent Georgian front, has an interesting octagonal stone-built dovecote. Inside, a ladder revolves on a wooden central shaft around the serried nest-holes. A pigeon, homing here, brought the first news of the battle of Waterloo: so they say! In the grounds, rhododendrons impede access to the *Loughor waterfall*, which provided Hugh Hughes (*c.* 1815) with one of his most beautiful wood engravings in the *Beauties of Cambria*. There is a huge expanse of anthracite open-cast working on the Penygroes road and a new drift mine at *Cwmgwili*, farther south; also a new industrial estate near the limekilns.

LLANDYFAELOG [13] A large scattered parish traversed on its east side by the fast Carmarthen to Llanelli road. The village has a few houses and a pub, and the churchyard a fine collection of conifers. Dr David Davis, who assisted at the birth of Queen Victoria, is commemorated by a plaque in the church.

LLANDYFEISANT [14] The park of the Dynevor estate and farm-

land, on the edge of Llandeilo. The *Dynevor* family is lineally descended from Roderic the Great who claimed sovereignty of all Wales in the 9c. When he died Wales was divided into three separate kingdoms, and Dynevor castle became the residence of the Lords Rhys, princes of South Wales. The castle is on the edge of a precipice overlooking the northern bank of the Tywi. On the further, north side, the ground falls gently away, with easy access to the narrow ledge on which the castle stands. It was built by Welsh princes mainly in the 12 and 13c. It has later, more domestic, additions on the north side, by Sir Rhys ap Thomas (16c). It is also in excellent preservation. The present house, to the north of the castle, is of the 17c and has moulded Jacobean plaster ceilings on the ground floor. In 1857 the facing was added in the castellated style of the period (architect R. K. Penson). Magnificent woodlands.

LLANEDI [17] A large parish with industrial Pontardulais to the south and Ammanford to the north, and sparsely populated agricultural land in between. The *Loughor* river forms the county boundary. St Edith's church is off the main road. It was rebuilt in 1860 (architect, R. K. Penson) except for the 13c tower base and the mortuary chapel of the Penrys family. They lived at *Cwrtceidrim or Plas Mawr*, a medieval house, now a ruin.

LLANEGWAD [14] The narrow Cothi valley with its sheer wooded slopes forms most of this

Lime kilns, **Llandybie**

parish which runs up country north of the Tywi. The village, near the river bank, is a cluster of houses around a rebuilt 1849 church which is approached through a cobbled yard with a gnarled tree and a mounting block in the centre. The low-aisled and barrel-vaulted church has good Perpendicular windows, but is rather thrown out of balance by a 1903 tower and spire. Inside there is a contrast of stained glass: on the south wall of the nave a Kempe-style Annunciation, a rich 1870-ish representation of the Rose of Sharon and the lilies of the field, and a modern window with St Catherine of Siena and St Margaret of Scotland. A heavy brass chandelier surmounted by a bird hangs from the roof of each aisle. In the north of the parish lies the village of *Brechfa*, a settled group of bellcote church

(1891, architect Lingen Barker), fishing pub in the doldrums (1973), four-square rectory, and a comparatively large but derelict house, *Ty Mawr* with massive outside chimney; belonging, like much of the village, to the Tregeyb estate, Llandeilo. There is much evidence of the Forestry Commission in this wild, lovely district.

LLANELLI [17] The largest town in the county, its prosperity is largely dependent on industry (see Introduction). The character of the town centre has changed in the last few years, and is still changing. Pedestrian shopping precincts have replaced or transformed the Victorian, overcrowded street pattern; the old covered market—a glass-domed building erected originally for an

eisteddfod—is now under a four-storey multi-car park. Familiarity breeds affection for places like markets, and it is natural that stall-holders and customers should feel nostalgic about the change. Many old landmarks have gone, to the regret of some of the older inhabitants, including much of *Church Street* and the *Salutation Arms*, so well-known to supporters of Llanelli Rugby Club, which celebrated its centenary in 1972 with a victory over the All Blacks. In their place is a two-storey *Magistrates' Court* (architect J. M. Harries, Bridgend) in dark slatey bricks, and the foundations are being prepared for an adjacent Crown Court building (architect D. M. Jones, Department of the Environment). The Court House is in contemporary vertical-slatted style. But the 1895 *Town*

45

Vanished,
and vanishing
Llanelli

Hall remains, a coherent balustraded, clocktower- and dome-topped example of civic architecture. So does *Congregational Tabernacle* opposite, compelling one's gaze to its Corinthian pillars, Palladian balustrade, and multiplicity of round-headed windows. Round the corner from the Town Hall comes a tall nondescript amusement building, and then the 1938 *Roman Catholic Church of Our Lady Queen of Peace* by W. S. Wort. Its lofty dark red brick angularities are relieved by the statue of the Madonna in painted Carrara marble. Six pairs of high pointed windows on each of the side walls flood the interior with light. The stained-glass war memorial windows above the gallery are by Patrick Feeny of the Hardman Studios, Birmingham. Each of these massive buildings has an air of detachment, and round them the one-way traffic swirls. The original parish church in Bridge Street is mostly by G. F. Bodley (1902) with tablets, mainly to the Stepney family, from the early 18c onwards, and Royal Arms of Queen Victoria. Opposite, *Llanelli House* dates from 1700 and has an imposing pattern of windows with cornices; it is the only building in the centre of the town of pre-20c architectural significance. One hopes that its preservation is assured. Away from the centre there are two or three late-Georgian houses in *Goring Road*; otherwise the architecture is entirely early Victorian, or later. The streets are properly laid out and the terraced houses, bright with new paint, look very well. Colonel E. Bruce Vaughan

47

Rhandir-mwyn lead mine **(Llanfair a'r y bryn)** before this valley became part of Llyn Brianne

designed the early 20c *Anglican Church* in *Alban road*, Sir Gilbert Scott the modest *St Paul's* (1857) off Ann Street, and G. E. Street *All Saints* (1874) in Goring Road, later lengthened and enlarged by A. E. Street. The splendour of All Saints is somewhat dimmed inside by an absence of light and the dark masonry of the walls, but it has style. These are some of the 30 or so places of worship in the borough. *Parc Howard*, now the property of Llanelli Town Council, covers 25 acres. It has a splendid show of flowers and shrubs and ample room for recreation. The house in the grounds, remodelled about 1885 by the Swansea architect

J. B. Wilson, has an art gallery and a museum of local interest with a collection of Llanelli pottery. It also assembles exhibitions by other museums. On the western outskirts towards Burry Port, *Kilymaenllwyd*, partly 17c, has been adapted to become a hospital and, near the famous rugby ground, *Stradey Castle*, standing in parkland, is a stone-built 18c house, with a west wing and tower added in 1874. Its interior has been altered but there is a suite of 18c rooms with scroll-worked ceilings on the ground floor. Here too, on the docks side is the plant of the *Llanelli Steel Company Ltd*, part of the Midland Duport Group, the largest of the steel com-

panies outside the British Steel Corporation. At the other end of the town, off the Swansea road, the *Trostre* steel plant is an impressive series of rectangular brick-built bays; one is half a mile long. *Cynheidre*, the largest of the anthracite collieries, is in the north of the rural parish.

LLANFAIR A'R Y BRYN [12] A483 enters the eastern part of the county at the *Sugar Loaf*, a hill which appears conical, but is in fact a short narrow ridge. From it there are views of the broken country leading into the Tywi valley and beyond. The road continues on the eastern flank of a valley ravine into the Bran valley through the village, little

more than a simple church (1883), an inn and a chapel, to the parish boundary on the outskirts of Llandovery. A minor road from Llandovery leads back into the wild country of the north, through the show village of *Rhandir-mwyn*, past the fine frontier farm of *Ystradffin*, noted for its Tywi Valley Pony Stud and Welsh Black Cattle and the tiny single-chamber church named after Peulin, Welsh variant of Paulinus. Founded in 1117, as an offshoot of Strata Florida to the north, it was rebuilt by the Cawdor family in 1821 and restored in 1900. Daniel Rowlands, curate of Llangeitho over the hills in Cardiganshire and one of the Welsh founders of Methodism, used it as a preaching house until the bishop intervened. The interior is sadly neglected (1973). Nearby, among the birch, boulders, and scrub oak, above the left bank of the Tywi is the cave of Twm Shon Catti, the Welsh Rob Roy, a picaresque 17c character. The cave is hard to find among the sheep tracks, but the scramble over the boulders can be fun on a fine day.

Beyond Ystradffin, the Tywi gorge is blocked by the glacier-like outer face of the *Llyn Brianne* reservoir dam, at its crest 290-ft above the valley floor. Built for the West Glamorgan Water Board and extending into Cardiganshire, the reservoir impounds the head waters of the Tywi and controls its subsequent flow as far as Nantgaredig between Llandeilo and Carmarthen;

Rhandir-mwyn,
Llanfair a'r y bryn

here pumps pass the water, drawn from the river, through a pipeline and tunnel into Glamorgan, where it is filtered. The reservoir (capacity 13,400 million gallons) is roughly the shape of a hand without the index finger, the middle finger pointing due north up the valley. In all about 7 miles of public roads have been built including a scenic route up the east side, but the county road from then on across the desert is not suitable for motor traffic, neither is motor traffic allowed on the Forestry road on the west side.

LLANFALLTEG EAST. *See* HEN-LLANFALLTEG.

LLANFIHANGEL ABERBYTH-YCH [14] The interest lies in the northern part, which is largely the estate and parkland of Golden Grove or Gelli Aur, one of the Welsh seats of the Cawdor family, now leased to the County Council as an Agricultural Training Institute. For generations this estate had been in the Vaughan family. Here Jeremy Taylor (1613–67), a friend of Richard Vaughan, second Earl of Carberry, and author of *Holy Living* and *Holy Dying*, found refuge from the Puritans after repeated imprisonment, once for publishing a catechism for children. In 1804 the eccentric John Vaughan left the estate to his friend, John Campbell of Stackpole, Pembs, first Earl of Cawdor. Golden Grove is an apt name for the beautiful woodland landscape on the southern slope of the Tywi valley, in which between 1826 and 1832 Sir Frederic Wyatville built the present mansion. Tudor Gothic in style

and splendidly built of stone blocks, soft-grey in tone, it has an imposing portico, large mullioned windows and stepped gables. A long, low, two-storey wing, closely windowed, extends along the west side and from the centre a lofty clock and bell turret rises, saddle-backed, dramatic in effect, but hardly in sympathy with the gentle landscape. The whole reminds one of one of those castles perched high above the valley of the Dordogne. Fine avenue of limes along the western drive.

LLANFIHANGEL ABERCYWYN. *See* ST CLEARS.

LLANFIHANGEL A'RARTH. [11] Once a quiet cross-roads village, but now getting strident with new building. The church is on the road north of the cross roads, past the raw looking *West Wales Central Electricity Depot*. 19c restoration has obliterated dateable features of the spacious two-chambered bellcote church of St Michael, which is divided down the centre by an arcade of four arches, with plenty of light through clear-glass windows. But there is antiquity in its weathered fabric and in a fine churchyard yew which has a stone bench round the trunk. Another centre of population is *Pencader*. Alongside a fast secondary road from Carmarthen to Cardigan Bay, it seems to have caught some of the fever of the traffic in its garish new houses which damp one's appreciation of the more self-assured, older buildings. There is a gaiety in the façade of the *Congregational Tabernacle* (1650/1909), in apricot and deep cream with gilt lettering. The early 19c Inde-

pendent chapel near the station, rebuilt on the site of a 17c chapel, probably the oldest in the county, is no longer a place of worship.

LLANFIHANGEL CILFARGEN. *See* LLANGATHEN.

LLANFIHANGEL RHOSYCORN [11] This is the centre of the *Brechfa Forest*, which can be seen at close range from the road running north into moorland through this wild and lovely parish. As it climbs through the Forest the lane is bordered, for amenity, with deciduous trees and Lawson's Cupressus. At *Pant y Bettws*, high above the Clydach valley and the hamlet of *Gwernogle*, is St Michael's church, a small primitive building with stone-flagged floors, clear-glass windows and, against the centre of the north wall, a small 18c pulpit; its front and back panels are each decorated with a gilded sunflower head carved in relief. Its nine members obviously care much for this delightful little church.

LLANFIHANGEL UWCH GWILI. *See* ABERGWILI.

LLANFYNYDD [14] Attractive village in a valley and hillside cobweb of lanes. The church (13c, with 15c north aisle) was simply restored in 1861 and the Perpendicular windows look well in the grey weathered walls. West tower with doorway the best feature. Inside, some interesting tablets in chancel, two steps below nave level. The village inn, *Pen y bont*, has a dance floor. On the hill south of village, *Farmers Arms*, brown, rough-cast, panelled in white, and 1839 Methodist chapel with long greenish ripply glass windows, make a good group. The high road north to Abergorlech takes you out into open country with staggering views of valleys and lower hills.

LLANGADOG [15] A4069 winds gently over the wooded valley floor until it starts the climb over the bare limestone slopes of the Black Mountains past old quarries and down into the industrial Amman valley; surely one of the most spectacular journeys in the kingdom. Llangadog is more than a village by Welsh standards. It has a close cluster of houses and hotels, and an expanse of common on its southern side. The church was completely rebuilt except for the tower in 1889, and the chancel recently refurnished and refloored. Stained glass by Walter Tower and R. J. Newberry. *Capel Gwynfe*, a hamlet in the middle of the parish, has a church of rusticated sandstone blocks and a low turreted tower, by E. H. Burton. It replaces an adjacent 1812 building of which the shell is left. Startling contrast between recent and older tombstone styles much to the favour of the latter, one of which serves as a stile. Superb countryside.

Garn Goch, an Iron Age hill fort, is on a high open ridge easily reached by car from *Bethlehem* village. There is a brisk trade before Christmas at minute Bethlehem Post Office in stamps and postmarks.

LLANGAIN [13] Where the Carmarthen/Llanstephan road rubs shoulders with the Tywi, Green Castle is the site of an Elizabethan mansion. Off the main road the church (1871, architect Stephen Lewis) stands on an old site. Simple and light, it has a painted stone reredos flanked by tiled memorials to the Gwyn family.

In the extreme north of the parish below A40, *Llanllwch* hamlet, of trim old cottages, lies in a pretty valley, now rather dominated from above by a bungalow estate of many colours. Except for the squat tower and outer walls of the chancel, the church has been rebuilt and a north aisle added.

LLANGATHEN [14] The remains of *Dryslwyn Castle*, slight and tumbled, are on a green knoll—obviously a prehistoric site—with the Tywi winding below it in the middle of the flat, verdant valley. The disposition of the flanking lines of hills and hillocks has made it one of the classic picturesque sites of Wales, celebrated by poets and painters since the start of the 18c. Paxton's tower (*see* Llanarthney) is to the south-west. Grongar Hill stands somewhat forward from the northern line of hills. John Dyer's poem, *Grongar Hill*, written at Aberglasney in 1726, still appears in anthologies. It has some of the intense romanticism that enlivens the best English art from Alexander Cozens to Samuel Palmer and beyond; the capacity to see all nature and experience during complete, immediate absorption by one small, representative thing, *seen* as for the first and only time.

Aberglasney, a big Georgian house encloses the remains of a

pp52/53 Pattern and texture ▷ The country at Bethlehem, near **Llangadog**

16c Bishop's Palace. Unoccupied, it is seen from half way up Grongar Hill. The sturdy church above Aberglasney has a 13c tower, a Tudor altar table, Jacobean communion rails, and Bishop Rudd's early 17c tomb with effigies. There is a sensible balance of clear and stained glass. (Among the latter, Faith Hope and Charity, by Cain Studios, Birmingham.) Yorkshireman Antony Rudd, Bishop of St David's from 1594 to 1614, bought Aberglasney; he preached a sermon before Queen Elizabeth which pleased her so much that there was talk of his becoming Archbishop of Canterbury, but he ruined his chances by a later sermon to the same audience in which he dwelt on the infirmities of old age, illustrating them by reference to the features of his congregation.

At Llanfihangel Cilfargen, on the other side of A40, Court Henry stands out clearly in a setting of woodland and pasture. The original house was built by Henry ap Gwilym in 1450, and although it was rebuilt in 1830 as a two-storeyed, plain-fronted Georgian house with short, narrow wing projections, medieval bits, e.g. windows, remain at the back. The adjacent, towered church on the hill is modern, and there is a pretty, lattice windowed village school on the valley floor below.

LLANGELER [10] A large scattered parish which includes the church parishes of Velindre and Penboyr. At *Henllan*, where

the road to Cardiganshire is carried on an ancient and narrow stone bridge, there is a fine river view of rocks and pools. Nearby *Llysnewydd*, designed by John Nash about 1800 and considerably altered about 70 years later, was demolished in 1972. Velindre is the main centre of population; it was once well known for its woollen mills of which two are now left. A valley road through Cwmpengraig runs to Penboyr and on to the rather sullen moorland on the road to Cynwyl Elfed. In this uphill country there are many barrows or tumuli dating from about 1500 B.C., shown on the Ordnance maps by the prefix "Crug".

Llangeler, *Velindre* and *Penboyr* parish churches are all mid to late 19c and of little interest; the first two were designed by C. J. Davies and D. Brandon

respectively. Penboyr churchyard is enclosed in a 6-ft high wall, built in 1809; so was its imposing block stone lychgate in classical style with a boarded barrel roof. The church has a floreated knob on a stone spirelet. Opposite the west gate, *Tomenllawdog*, a partly excavated mound may be the site of a motte castle.

Pentrecourt, near Llandyssul, is another centre of population; here also there are two woollen mills.

The upland landscape here, as in all north west Carmarthenshire has hundreds of laburnum trees in the hedgerows, well away from habitation. They are at their best in June.

On the western boundary of the parish, where the top road from Newcastle Emlyn to Carmarthen via Hermon and Cyn-

The Tywi at Dryslwyn, ▷
(Llangathen)

wyl Elfed comes near to open country, there is a large bracken covered mound, *Tomenseba*, probably a Norman or Welsh Motte Castle.

LLANGENNECH [17] On the Loughor estuary between Llanelli and Swansea, once a rich coal area but now largely residential.

LLANGLYDWEN. *See* CILY-MAENLLWYD and LLAN-BOIDY.

LLANGUNNOR [14] *"Behold Llangunnor leering o'er the Vale"*: opening line of a poem, *The Head of the Rock*, on a tablet in the church to Sir Richard Steele, "author of the immortal essays named Tatlers, Guar-

Aberglasney, **Llangathen**

dians and Spectators". Sir Richard Steele spent his last days at *Ty Gwyn*, a plain farmhouse outside Carmarthen. It belonged to his second wife, "dear Prue", and on her death, and burial in Westminster Abbey, he left London for good. The parish, beyond the river from Carmarthen, has no village nucleus. The bellcote church, alone except for the vicarage and small farm buildings, stands on a hillside, with a view to the east down the green Tywi valley. Its foundation is 13c and the original church seems to have been what is now the south aisle. Later an aisle, now the main nave and chancel, was added on the north side. A thorough restoration took place in 1815, as seen in the block arrangement of the boxed pews and the round slender columns between the two aisles. Stone-flagged floor except for the tiled sanctuary; 1932 stained glass by Webb at the west end and, more recent by Celtic Studios in the east end windows. A stone slab, gracefully incised with one cross inside another is well mounted on a sill in the porch. A very well tended church, inside and out.

LLANGYNDEYRN [14] An open village of aloofly sited houses in the Gwendraeth Fach valley, with a slight feeling of industry from the Gwendraeth Fawr anthracite valley over the hill ridge to the south. Very white farms against very green banks, and limestone quarries evident on the hillside. The 13c church, partly rebuilt in 1884, has a slender tower, defaced by ugly openings in the upper storey. But the outside has more sympathetic colour and texture than most in the county, and the walls inside have not been ruined by scraping or cementing. Refurbishing of course, and there is sad, green, ripply glass. 1676 woodwork between chancel and north aisle.

LLANGYNIN [13] A pocket handkerchief parish to the west of and above the Cynin valley; a few scattered farms and a towered medieval church off the road down to A40. It is virtually deserted, and sadly needing repair. An arcade of three rough pointed arches separates an empty south aisle. Stone-flagged floors.

LLANGYNOG [13] A deeply rural parish; the double lines of electricity pylons which traverse the southern part of the county are specially in evidence. *Coomb*, the first Cheshire Home in Wales, is an attractive, stone-built, early 20c, three-storeyed house with gables and a square tower block barely above the roof line, at the east end. It formerly belonged to Lord Kylsant. The dolmen, *Twlc y Viliast* (Greyhound's Kennel), is completely hidden in brambles at the edge of the large, working quarry below the school near Ebenezer chapel. *Llandeilo Abercowyn* is a remote farm on the east bank of the Taf estuary. The church in the farmyard is now an ivy-draped Cotmanesque byre. The farm has a 15c wheel-shaped window in the east wall.

LLANLLAWDOG [14] A road branches off A485, nine miles or so north of Carmarthen, and eastward to the forest land of Brechfa. Bordered by beech trees, it winds along the northern bank of the upper Gwili valley. By its side and keeping company with a copper beech tree, the parish church is simple in an early Victorian style. The three tall lancet windows on each side of the nave have, with one exception, clear glass in leaded panes. The exception is a modern Christ in Majesty window by John Hayward dedicated to John and Mary Bowen Davies, whose portraits are included in a roundel in the bottom corner, John in barrister's wig and gown. The late 19c glass of the Ascension at the west end is in a tenderer, less arresting idiom.

LLANLLWCH. *See* LLANGAIN.

LLANLLWNI [11] From the bridge in the north of the parish on the county boundary, you can see trout rising in the dark pools of the Teifi far below. The church on a knoll among enclosing hills has a typical tall west end tower, slightly tapered, and is a blend of 13 and 20c work. The churchyard has an array of shiny black tombstones and Irish yews. The chancel and nave were sympathetically restored in the 1930s and the original altar stone, a rough boulder with three consecration crosses, was put back. Clear glass throughout, except for a mid 19c east window and Kempe-style 1936 stained glass over the private pew of *Maesy-crugiau Manor*. The latter, now a hotel, was rebuilt about 1904, but not to the whole design of the architect, Arnold Mitchell. It has a high corbelled tower and stands in a park.

LLANNON [14] The village centre, a few houses, the Plas, a wayside inn, and the tree-shaded church, is on the A476 Llanelli to Llandeilo road, and another good road leads due south to Hendy on the county boundary near Swansea. Although industrial Swansea is so near, the feeling is quite rural. All that is left of the medieval church is the plain 14c tower at the west end. The rest was rebuilt by E. Haycock in 1831 when the two aisles were converted into a roomy, single chamber; the nave roof was flattened but the chancel has an elegant, almost ogee, panelled roof. Early English-style windows high above ground level with clear glass, plastered walls, Celtic Studio stained glass in east end windows. The hatchment on the south wall is of the Griffiths family of Marchoglwyn, which no longer exists. Otherwise a featureless interior.

LLANPUMPSANT [13] The five Celtic saints to whom the church is dedicated, and who give the village its name ("five-saint-church"), are Ceitho, Celynnin, Gwyn, Gwyno and Gwynoro. There are substantial late 18 and early 19c houses at the northern end of the village, which is quartered by the Gwili river running in one direction and the Carmarthen to Aberystwyth railway track in the other. The best part is near the church, where large farm buildings and cottages make a compact group on a winding road. Much of the church was rebuilt in 1882. It has a pleasant 1939 stained glass east window by Muriel Minter, from drawings by Elsie Eldridge, dedicated in

Welsh to a former vicar, and outlines of each of the five saints are incised and painted on panels in the oak reredos. A good straight road runs from the village north towards Llandyssul and Cardiganshire.

LLANSADURNEN. *See* LLANDOWROR.

LLANSADWRN [15] One is captivated by the setting of this village grouped around a large walled churchyard, but saddened by the present air of neglect and dereliction. The long, ugly, bellcote church has been so restored and altered that its antiquity is conjectural. The blocked doorway at the west end suggests an earlier tower. The porch on the south side has a simple pointed archway, repeated in the entrance to the church; perhaps 13c. There are signs of small 15c windows, and what is now the vestry, to the south of the chancel, may once have been a chapel. There is a small pound at the southern entrance to the churchyard next to the War Memorial and, due north, almost against the churchyard, stone-built *Ebenezer Congregational Chapel* (1874). With its bull's eye and long gallery windows it broods over the village. Northwest, at *Waun Clydfa*, the 1841 Baptist Chapel *Libanus* (this relic of the Roman for Lebanon is not uncommon in Wales) peeps out from behind a monkey puzzle tree, in its original state. *Abermarlais*, hidden in parkland on A40 in the south of the parish, was rebuilt early in the 19c for Admiral Foley who led the fleet at the Battle of the Nile. (*See* also Llawhaden, Pembs.)

LLANSAINT. *See* ST ISHMAELS.

LLANSAWEL [11] An unspoilt village grouped around a simple church with squat west tower and 13c lancet windows. Extensively restored in the 1860s. At the eastern entrance to the village *Castle Green* is a square, Georgian, two-storeyed house with well arranged upper and lower sash windows and a simple pediment porch with Doric pillars. The principal house *Edwinsford*, on the Cothi, is now derelict. There is talk of its partial restoration. Access to the grounds is restricted, as subsidiary buildings are privately occupied. The main house, to be seen from the road, is 17c with large later additions. *Glan yr Annell*, a Nash-type house of *c.* 1800, now a hotel, stands in rich parkland. Extensive quarrying of *Pen y Ddinas* has left the peak of this outcrop looking sphinx-like from a distance.

LLANSTEPHAN [13] The Norman Castle is romantically sited on a promontory between the Taf and the Tywi estuaries. It rises from a green knoll, above a fringe of woodland like a monk's tonsure, and, as seen from sea level on the north side it is the beau ideal of an 18c engraving. On what was probably an Iron Age fort the Normans first built a pallisaded motte and bailey castle. The earliest buildings to replace it are the late 12c walls of the Upper Ward in the south-east corner. Its most imposing feature is the great Gatehouse on the north side, part of the Edwardian refortification at the end of the 13c. The castle changed hands frequently dur-

Llanstephan

ing the Welsh uprisings but the Welsh never held it for any length of time in face of the Norman/English control of the sea. To-day, though parking is severely frowned on anywhere between the village and the castle, which is now under the care of the Department of the Environment, the ascent is worth it for its own sake and for the view of the Carmarthen hills, Gower coast and stretches of golden, cockled, sands. At sea level, the village houses and shops have a tranquil Victorian air, and the greensward (as it would be called in Frinton) between the terraced cottages and the sea gives plenty of elbow room. Principal houses are *Plas*, remodelled in 1788 on earlier foundations in the Greek

Revival style, and at the other end *The Cottage*, now a hotel. The church has lots of character. Restored and repewed in 1872 it has transepts with wide, low, pointed arches, massive walls, early 19c wall tablets (in the chancel), and (in the chancel chapel) interesting 17 and 18c tombs enclosed in low iron grills, two hatchments of the Meares family of Plas, and a shallow Norman font. The nave is low, and darkened by late 19c stained glass, some very tender. Stone-flagged floor. East window by Celtic Studios. Against the churchyard wall the village pound has been roofed, and is now a sweetshop. In the hamlet of *Llanybri* where farmyards, open to the road, impart a French rustic flavour, the cha-

pel, dedicated to the Virgin, is now a ruin. It was a chapel of ease to Llanstephan, and handed over to the Dissenters by an agent of the Duke of Northumberland who, among other benefices in the south of the county, had that of Llanstephan. Fox hounds from neighbouring farms roam the village streets. They are hunted on foot and are reputed to be deadly.

LLANWINIO [13] Church on the Meidrim to Cardigan road is modern and of no interest. The parish, a rough quadrilateral on a north–south axis, is divided by valleys and streams draining south to the Tywi plain. They make east to west travel interesting, through the valleys of *Cwmbach* where there

Newcastle Emlyn

is a pretty chapel and school group, and *Cwmfelin Mynach*, where Baptist Ramoth chapel (1907) stands out.

LLANWRDA [15] The narrow bridge on A40 has now been by-passed. The road north to Lampeter winds through some of the finest valley and upland scenery in south Wales.

LLANYBRI. *See* LLAN-STEPHAN.

LLANYBYTHER [11] A small and pleasant enough market town among the undulations flanking the Teifi valley, it is noted for its horse sales, claimed to be the biggest in the kingdom, and held on the last Thursday of each month.

Buyers from all over the country and abroad attend the sales and the number of horses that change hands at each sale is rarely less than two hundred. They are now mainly hunters and ponies. There is a fine road south to Llansawel through hilly country, much of which forms part of the State Forest of Brechfa. The church has a squat old tower, but was uninter-estingly Victorianized. ("Cath-edral" stained glass in east win-dow.) Low, stone-built *Cross Hands Hotel* is the best building, amid some decent colour-washed houses. Brown stucco chapel, *"Aberduar"*. Woollen Mills at *Rhyd y bont* on Llan-sawel road. Southward, *Aber-gorlech* village is full of charm and character. The three-arched angle-buttressed bridge over the Gorlech may be the oldest in the county. On the river bed lie curiously worn turtleback stones. Quoit tournaments are all the rage, the quoits being hand-forged locally, and coloured or silvered. Simple church (1885, architect Lingen Barker) with splendid hanging brass paraffin lamps. The gayest of cottages, and plain white-plastered Con-gregational chapel of 1822. Fine valley road to Brechfa.

LLANYCRWYS [12] Sparse upland parish with modest, well-cared-for single-chamber church, rebuilt about 1890 (architect Euan Christian), in the Twrch valley. Much more obtrusive is the stone-faced Con-gregational chapel of 1873 at *Ffald y Brenin*.

MARROS. *See* EGLWYS CYMYN.

MEIDRIM [13] There is a very pretty valley road from St Clears to the centre of this attractive and mature village set on a hillside, and grouped around the junction of two secondary roads, important as alternatives to A40 for traffic to and from the north coast. The Methodist chapel has a spec-

tacular front of grey stone blocks, freestone pilasters at each corner and turrets. The simple church in an oval on a prehistoric site was rebuilt about 100 years ago. The inside is dull; it has an 18c tablet to the Rice Thomas family. Outside the stone lychgate is a modest but well disposed row of single storey cottages with pointed doorways. From the lychgate to the church door is an arched avenue of yew trees.

MERTHYR [13] A simple church by R. K. Penson and little else. Do not take the road shown on the Ordnance Survey map leading off A40 past Derllys Court (modern farm-house). It ends in another farm-yard. *Cana* Congregational cha-pel (1821–62) stands on A40 and you see through the long clear-glass windows on either side.

MYDDFAI [15] In the foothills of the Black Mountains and in a countryside notable for its oak trees growing singly, as it were in parkland, or in rows along hedges. A few cottages and an inn are grouped round a 13c church, which is one of the best in the county, in spite of the usual disasters. The east end of the north aisle is boarded off to form a vestry, obscuring a medieval window. (The next window to it has bits of medie-val glass.) The southern aisle, now nave, is 15c. Most of the windows are original and clear-glazed. Floor of stone flags (except for the tiled chancel). Barrel-vaulted roofs, with pat-tern of timber ribs. Gwynne Holford hatchment. Modern brass tablet, north of altar,

obscures an 18c wall-painting of the Prayer of Consecration. *Cil-gwyn*, once the Gwynne Holford seat, is a plain 18c building of three storeys with good window arrangement, and particularly good balustrading to the origi-nal wide oak staircase. Parts of it are decayed beyond repair, and its whole future is un-certain. The adjacent out-buildings are in separate occu-pation.

Myddfai is famous—or should be so—for a line of physi-cians and veterinary surgeons who practised hereabouts until the 1880s including Rees Williams M.D., who died an old man in 1842. Folklore says that the line started with Rhiw-allon, the eldest of three sons of the marriage between a mortal farmer and a fairy of Llyn y fan fach (*see* Llanddeusant). They lived at *Esgair Llaethdy*, still a farmhouse in the parish. There is a place near the house called *Pant y Meddygon* (Physician's Dingle).

The village should also be famous among Welshmen for Morgan Owen, who lies buried on the north side of the church chancel. One of the great churchmen of Wales, chaplain of Archbishop Laud, he built the porch of St Mary's church, Oxford, and, persecuted by Puritans, he died in the parish in 1644.

NEWCASTLE EMLYN [10] A small town and the market centre for much of south Cardi-ganshire and north Car-marthen and an important milk collection and processing centre. The castle lies to the east of the town; a gate and a few walls remain. It was built on an older site in the 15c by Sir Rhys ap Thomas, friend and sponsor of Henry VII, more as a country seat than as a fortress, but it served the latter purpose when it held out for the king in the Civil Wars, only to be demolished at the close. The site is picturesque and as yet unadministered by the Department of the Environment, on hillocks overlooking the river Teifi which pursues an eccentric course around three of its sides. The town, of little or no architectural or artistic interest, is a long street of variegated architecture, winding down to the angle-buttressed bridge on the Teifi. But it is a pleasant place, very Welsh, with friendliness and bustle rising to a crescendo on Friday, market day. A cul-de-sac off the main street leads to the church, the school, the Magistrates' Court and Methodist *Bethel* chapel. The church, down an avenue of lime trees, was built in the 1840s (architect J. L. Collard) and altered and enlarged 80 years later by W. D. Caröe. It is a plain nave and chancel building with good tower and porch and a slate sundial protruding from the south wall. Inside, the floor is paved with large slate slabs, matched by the slate stone of the square piers which carry the roof, and by the stone of the chancel arch. The modern font of polished slate looks well, standing free below the organ loft. Chairs take the place of pews. Clear glass in the nave allows plenty of light, and the walls carry two hatchments of the Hall family of Cilgwyn across the river in Cardiganshire. Stained glass in the east window is by Horace Wilkin-

son. Near the church, the single-storey *Magistrates' Court* of well-cut slate blocks is a baby clinic on Fridays. *Bethel* has fine proportions with its detached vestry, and now looks splendid in grey, picked out in blue. The 19c school, with later additions and playing field, complete a very attractive group in the Welsh idiom. Other chapels are *Congregational* (1880) with contrasting stone refacing and greyish classical *Baptist* with pedimented portico and façade.

NEWCHURCH [13] Overlooks Carmarthen town, in pleasantly wooded country. The 1829 church, off the main road, was simply restored in the 1870s and has two stained-glass windows of that period by Gibbs.

PEMBREY [16] Has suffered industrially, like Burry Port, from the eastward drift of industry towards the Swansea valley. Its chief potential asset is the enormous expanse of sandy sea shore on Carmarthen Bay. Although acres of devastated and ruined buildings separate it from the main coast road, paid access is possible immediately west of the point where the coast road is carried over the railway, north of the village. Now that the threat of a firing range has been removed, surely something will soon be done to make this area more attractive (*see* Introduction). The church in the centre of the village is late 13c with a northern aisle added shortly afterwards. Fine 16c timber barrel roof over the earlier part, and 17c communion rails. The four-light window in the south wall is 16c,

and the soffits are carved with emblems of the Passion and shields of arms. Stained glass by W. Wilkinson and Celtic Studios. The round-headed porch door carries the date 1717, and is a replica in date and design of that to the tower entrance inside Kidwelly church.

PENBOYR. *See* LLANGELER.

PENCADER. *See* LLANFIHANGEL a'r ARTH.

PENCARREG [11] The simple church is perched on top of a rock overlooking the Llanybyther to Lampeter road. It was rebuilt in 1878 and the stone has since weathered to a pleasant grey. The 12c font is carved roughly in relief on the round limestone basin with four heads, supposed to be those of Christ as a youth, a man, on the Cross and in Glory.

PENDINE [16] Wedged tightly at sea level between the Proof and Experimental Establishment of the Ministry of Defence at Llanmiloe to the east and massive cliffs to the west is a truly remarkable array of caravans, chalets, bungalows, amusement buildings and other amenities. It defies description. The Service buildings contribute nothing to the scene and the best that can be said for their layout and appearance is that, like the cliffs, they prevent further coastal sprawl. The lane banks up the hill behind are pervaded by winter heliotrope, with its aromatic smell, and the parish church on higher ground still is of no special interest. Sea bathing is excellent and the sands though restricted (*see* In-

Pembrey

troduction) are splendid. Fifty years or so ago, racing car drivers used them for testing and record breaking. Parry Thomas was killed on them in 1927 trying to regain the world speed record taken from him by Malcolm Campbell at 174 m.p.h. His twelve-cylinder car, which was left buried in the sands after his death, was dug up in 1971, and put back into running order, to be housed eventually in a special museum at Pendine.

PENTRECOURT. *See* LLAN-GELER.

PEN Y BONT. *See* TRELECH A'R BETWS.

PONTYBEREM [14] A mining village where roads converge in the Gwendraeth valley, now more dependent on new industries around Llanelli, and with no air of depression.

ST CLEARS or SANCLER [13] A traffic-worried market town on A40, the users of which see nothing of interest. But on the Laugharne road there are some simple Georgian and Victorian houses, a green and pleasant mound, low and bereft of its castle, and an old water-mill to give a bit of character. Here too the church has style, in an ample churchyard adorned by a weeping ash. It was the

church of a monastic cell in the 12c, which explains the elaborate Norman chancel arch with well-carved capitals—surprising for these parts. Otherwise plain inside, it has a lot of light from clear glass in deeply splayed windows, some early 20c stained glass, stone-flagged floors, and a circular Norman font. Organ loft in west gallery, and doors to the ten front pews. *Llanfihangel Abercywyn* is an ecclesiastical parish with a new (1900ish) church on A40 between Bancyfelin and St Clears. The old 13c church is to the south, roofless and ivy-covered, across the fields from *Trefenty Farm*, on the Taf estuary.

63

Talley Abbey

ST ISHMAELS [16] The lonely
13c church, beautifully sited
above the sheer rocks of the
Tywi estuary was restored in
1860 by R. K. Penson; he left
some features intact, the arcade
between the nave and north
aisle, an oblique passage from
the south transept to the chancel, and stone seats round the
sanctuary walls; but a screen
across the nave and north aisle
is disfiguring; so is the tiled
reredos. A vaulted porch, four
steps below the nave level,
forms the ground stage of the
saddleback tower which lost its

upper storey and familiar finish
of battlement and corbel in a
great storm. *Llansaint* is a hilltop
village of houses huddled
together around a circular
churchyard. On a miniature
scale it calls to mind Proust's description of Combray—"no
more than a church epitomising
a town, representing it, speaking of it and for it to the horizon
... as a shepherd gathers his
sheep, the woolly grey backs of
its flocking houses". Between
Llansaint and sea level are huge
concrete poultry houses, and at
sea level *Tan y lan* farmhouse

has a neat front elevation of
square sash windows. The farm
buildings of block stone were
built as model buildings by the
landowner, the Earl of Cawdor,
about 100 years ago. The cockle
women still come down from
Llansaint and leave their tak-
ings in baskets outside the farm
to be collected by lorry.

This large parish also includes *Ferryside*, where the main
coast road and the Paddington
to Fishguard railway run alongside the Tywi estuary. It is
becoming more and more
popular as a seaside resort,

although as yet hardly developed. *St Thomas' church* is a period (1876) piece of Welsh architecture inside and out. Good Victorian and modern houses on rising ground towards St Ishmaels. *Iscoed*, a square red-brick Georgian mansion from which Sir Thomas Picton rode to his death at Waterloo, has been demolished.

TALLEY [12] All that remain of the *Augustinian Abbey* founded in the 12c by the Welsh prince Rhys ap Gruffydd (for the Premonstratensian or Reformed Canons) are the gaunt high-pointed arches at the east end of the nave and the entrance to the north transept. You see these, but you feel to the full the sense of peace and seclusion which brought the monks to this valley with its two lakes and rich pastures. Now trim cottages, a farm, and, to one side, a Georgian house set among soaring conifers and beeches, adjoin the west boundary of the Abbey grounds. To the north, divided by a Department of the Environment wire fence, is the simple bellcote church, built in 1772. The lakes are beyond. The church has kept its oak boxed-in pews, clear glass windows and stone-flagged floor. The pews are numbered and set in chapel fashion, with a solid block in the centre and smaller blocks forming north and south aisles. At *Cwmdu* the road narrows, bordered on one side by a stream and on the other by a curious row of four cottages painted apricot, two-storeyed with lower windows in round headed recesses, alternately blocked. *Cwmdu Inn* is at one end and *Baptist Providence chapel*

(1789/1883) at the other. The chapel key is readily available at the first cottage and the tiny interior is well worth looking at, for its tiered seating, gallery, absurdly gaily painted ceiling and gallery support pillars, marbled iron with capitals to match the ceiling. Hanging lantern with coloured-glass panels in vestibule. Westward at *Pant Soar* cross roads a sister Baptist chapel has been elegantly converted into a private house.

TRELECH A'R BETWS [13] A scattered parish of hamlets and isolated buildings, typical of the heart of the county and approached from the north by a moorland road from Maudsland to St Clears. The eastern boundary is partly the narrow and beautiful sylvan *Cynin valley* which is closely seen from the road from Velindre to Gelliwen. *Congregational Rock Chapel*, rebuilt and enlarged in 1827, dominates the cross roads hamlet of *Trelech*. It has the conventional two entrance doors, well-shaped windows, good masonry and an outside staircase to the gallery. The only church in the parish is on a hill overlooking the hamlet of *Pen y bont* in the steep Dewi Fawr valley; hardly worth the risk of finding it locked, so tucked away is it. It was built in 1834 by David Morgan, and Goodhart Rendel in his card index of Victorian churches (rarely flattering to such modest buildings) calls it 'an outrageously mean little chapel'. But it is light, with clear white walls. A Benefaction Board records two bequests, one in 1788 by William Davies of London, as well as carrying a painting of an

early 19c schoolroom, schoolmaster and mistress attending to their charges, some on benches and others at desks.

VELINDRE. *See* LLANGELER.

WHITLAND [6] On the county boundary: the tradesmen's entrance to Pembrokeshire. A small market town with little or no apparent personality to users of A40 but it is the centre of a large milk-producing area and Unigate Limited provides much local employment. Because of a steady increase in milk production in the surrounding districts, its creamery can now handle up to 140,000 gallons of milk a day. This compensates to some extent for the town's loss of importance as a railway junction, when the branch line to Cardigan was closed. In the centre of the town, the *Fishers Arms Hotel* is popularly held to be the site to which clerics and laity were summoned about 940 A.D. by Hywel Dda (Howell the Good, King of all Wales) to codify the Welsh Law. The *Cistercian Abbey of Alba Landa* (*White Land*) lay about a mile north of the town in the Gronow valley. A late-Victorian house now stands near the site and nothing of the Abbey stands above ground. There were iron-works at the junction of the Gronow and Nant Colomendy in the 17c. They closed about 1800. The church, modest and mid-Victorian, is south of the town near a low three-arched bridge of some age over the Taf. The stained glass in the south chancel window is by Walter Tower and the 1853 east window is richly coloured.

Pembrokeshire: Introduction

Stones, the sea and the weather have moulded the look of Pembrokeshire. Man has merely scratched its surface.

Things that strike the visitor because they are likely to be a change to his eyes are the stone walls and the earth banks which enclose the fields, the fine, bleached grass, bushes and small trees, gorse, hawthorn and oak, often blown into strange shapes. And in winter the tall, pale trunks of bigger trees, beech and sycamore, near white or pink-walled farms, the slurried roofs and the sheets

◁ Part of the stone alignment at **Llanllawer** and (*below*) St Davids Head

of snowdrops marking the sites of dwellings of which no other traces remain. Then the thin, clear light and the stretches of undeveloped seaboard, the fierce romantic cliffs with their caves and contortions, and the many beaches difficult or impossible to get to and the few with wide sands, and blue-grey pebble banks.

Agriculture is the county's industry; urban land is only 3 per cent. Over an area no larger than Greater London, the varieties of soil structure and climate are surprising. In the south of the county the soil is mainly red sandstone like that of Devon and Brecon. Very fertile, it grows heavy crops but, if it

has a drawback, it is that it is not so easily worked after rain as the soil in the north. In the extreme south-west, layers of coal-bearing limestone are easily seen in the cliff scenery, and in the stones on the beaches round Angle, and the quarried product in the pillars of Castlemartin and other churches.

The north has three distinct patterns of soil and fertility—the Preseli hills and foothills, deficient in lime and suitable for forestry and summer grazing for sheep and mountain ponies; the coastal strip, nowhere more than three miles deep, from Fishguard round St David's Head to Broadhaven, where it meets the red sandstone; finally the interior, and area east of Fishguard, sound, unexciting land, abundant in grass and dairy herds. The northern coastal strip is treeless, windswept and stony, sheltered by banks of stone and earth or by blown hedges shaped like horses' manes. Its soil, largely volcanic in origin, is among the most fertile in Britain. Battered in winter by Atlantic gales, it looks very different in spring, and by early June it is as

◁ Ruined village near **St Davids**
below **Treffgarne**

Pattern and texture: seaside farms **St Nicholas** 71

p74 St Govan's Head, **Bosherston** ▷
p75 Pwllcrochan, **St Nicholas**

colourful as an Alpine meadow. The cliffs are rock gardens in full bloom of sedum, thrift, gorse and thyme all among lichen-mottled boulders; the hedgerows herbaceous borders of ferns, foxgloves and other wayside flowers. To farm here is like farming in a flower pot of chosen compost, and the quality of the farming (for instance round Mathry) is worthy of the soil. There are farms which in production per acre of straightforward farming equal, and can exceed, any in Britain. Almost all crops come alike to it. The four- or five-year leys produce highest quality grass but it is, par excellence, arable country famed for its corn as far back as Tudor days. It is also ideal early potato land.

Climate is as important as the soil, and as varied. The coastal rainfall of 30 inches or so a year increases inland with every mile. Frosts are rare and so is the dry hot sunshine not infrequent in England. Barley of malting sample cannot be grown, nor can winter-sown corn. So though spring is early, harvest is late. Strangely, the land seems to rest about July. Growth ceases for some weeks. In August it starts again, and goes on well into November. There is a great flush of autumn grass valuable to the dairy farmer, and often round Michaelmas a spell of fine weather. The Welsh of the north call these periods the August Spring and the Small Summer of Michaelmas.

Few farms have more than 300 acres; the average is less than 150. The pattern of the countryside is curious, one of isolated farms and cottages linked by a labyrinth of rural roads, restricted in width by land hunger. This is specially true of the north where, up to the time of Henry VIII, land was fragmented by inheritance laws. The rural population is a fraction of what it was 100 years ago; thousands of cottages have gone.

Soil, climate and modern transport to fetch and carry: these are the basic elements of farming success. Originally, the county was more fortunate than most in its sea communications, and in ports such as Milford, Haverfordwest and Fishguard, supplemented by innumerable coves where limestone and coal were landed and farm produce loaded; hence the number of limekilns near the beaches, and ruined storehouses as at Abercastle and Newport. Railways reached Tenby, Haverfordwest and Pembroke in the 1860s, and Fishguard in 1906, but were never extended to the rich area of St Davids or Newport. Late in the 19th century a single line, now closed, ran from Clynderwen to Letterston, where an important cattle market developed. To-day lorries carry cattle and farm produce to near and distant markets, a far cry from the days of the drovers. The milk lorry symbolises the backbone of farming in all of west Wales. The creation of the Milk Marketing Board in the 1930s was as important here as the Repeal of the Corn Laws in 1846. Thirty-five years ago, rabbit trapping made up much of the farmers' income. To-day it is grass, cheapest to produce and the cow's favourite food. Pembrokeshire, with its good land and rainfall, produces it in enormous quantities.

The outline of the county from Cemaes Head in the north-west round to Milford Haven roughly resembles that of Wales itself, upper and lower jaws protruding from an open mouth, with an extra chin below the Haven, which is a tidal channel into the heart of the county as far as Haverfordwest, the county town. The twin rivers, Eastern and Western Cleddau, which rise in and near the Preseli hills flow south into it, gathering tributaries on their way, and together, as Daugleddau, form an estuary of really outstanding beauty and variety in woodland and marsh.

The north-east corner of the county is dominated by the Preseli hills, the westward-declining limb of the Cambrian range. The foothills come close to the sea between Fishguard and Newport.

◁ **Llangloffan**   73

Though no point in the county is more than ten miles from salt water, the magnificent coast line runs for 170 miles, and the whole can be walked from St Dogmaels to Amroth. The coastal strip is a National Park: so are the Preseli hills. The coastal walk gives the chance to see, in the cliff faces, the great variety of rock and rock-formation; the shale of the north-west and the cavernous folds on Cemaes Head, the igneous purple rocks around St Davids, the red sandstone chimneys over Marloes beach, and the great limestone cliffs of the south coast from St Govan's Head to Lydstep. The Preseli hills are dealt with in more detail in the gazetteer, as are the offshore islands (*see* Skokholm).

The people are of mixed blood; what their ancestors have left above ground confer on the county a special character. The dolmens and remains of burial chambers mark the passage of the megalith builders 5,000 or so years ago along their western trade routes.

St Ann's Head, **Dale**

Marloes

p78 Pwllcrochan, **St Nicholas**
p79 Bullslaughter Bay, **Bosherston** ▷

Carreg Samson, **Mathry**

Most of these are in the north of the county; the more dramatic are those which stand high on the forehead of the land facing the sea, Trellys (St Nicholas) and Pentre Ifan (Nevern). The latter is worth seeing if only for the delicate poise of its capstone. A close but broken alignment of standing stones at Llanllawer suggest the processional route to a burial chamber or circle, long since vanished. The Bronze Age men have left 100 or so barrows, evenly distributed; and their successors the Celts, the hill fort refuges, notably Carn Ingli and Garn Fawr, and their language, still more widely used in the north of the county than English. But in physical characteristics, the tall, fair-haired Celts are not so prominent as the short, dark-haired men of the megaliths.

There are no traces of Roman occupation, and the next invaders were the Vikings or Norsemen. They came to raid and plunder, mainly from bases on the east coast of Ire-

Pentre Ifan, **Nevern**

land, but gradually they came to terms with the Welsh and eventually to help them in their struggles against the English; but this was a long process, and in the 10th century St Davids was sacked four times by Vikings. Evidence of their colonies is in such place names as Fishguard, Goodwick, Skomer and Skokholm.

The only outward signs of the Dark Ages and the early Christian period are the incised stones and crosses, which Dr V. E. Nash-Williams in his authoritative book *Early Christian Monuments in Wales* puts into three main groups—the simple inscribed stones from the 5th to the 7th centuries A.D. including those with Latin/Ogam inscriptions,* the cross

*Ogam is a script or cypher used by visiting Irish Celts. Letters are represented by a series of notches in groups of 1 to 5, cut at different angles on either side of the sharp edges of a stone. By these variations an alphabet of 25 letters was devised. There are good examples at Nevern.

81

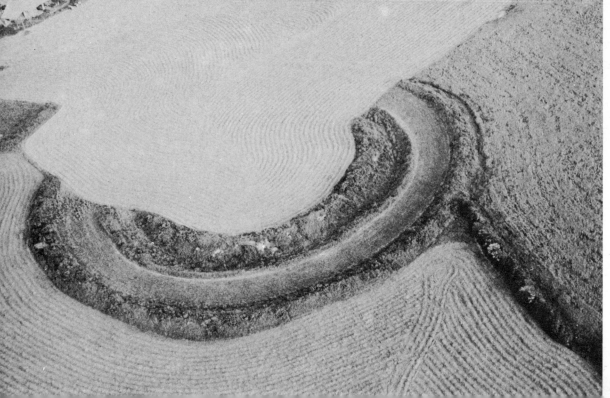

Foel Drygarn (**Whitechurch**)

decorated stones from the 7th to the 9th centuries, and the standing sculptured crosses from the 9th to the 11th centuries. There are more in total in Pembrokeshire than in any other Welsh county, and there are more in the north than in the south. Llanwnda, for example, has four from the first two groups built into the fabric of its church and one lying in the churchyard. Elaborately sculptured crosses of the 10th and 11th centuries can be seen at Nevern in the north, and at Carew and Penally in the south. Dr Nash-Williams suggests that the sudden appearance of this developed sculpture in Wales is

due to the settling of differences between the Celtic and Latin churches in the 8th century, the consequent renewal of contact between Wales and England, and an influx of craftsmen from, e.g. Northumbria (*see* Penally). Standing as high as thirteen feet above the ground as at Carew and Nevern, their wheel-heads, usually mortise and tenon jointed to the shafts, they are intricately carved on all faces with abstract and sometimes naturalistic patterns. Slab crosses, as at Carew and Penally, differ from the pillar cross at Nevern in that their width greatly exceeds their thickness.

◁ Castell Mawr rath (**Eglwyswrw**) and (*below*) Keeston rath (**Camrose**)

Llanwnda Llanychllwydog Llanychllwydog

St Non's Chapel (**St Davids**) Llanwnda Mathry

84 **Carew** cross and detail ▷

St Davids

The Norman invaders spread along the south coast and drove the Welsh from the fertile lands up to, .and beyond, the Preseli range. Having secured their base with a chain of castles, Roch, Wiston, Llawhaden, Narberth and Amroth—a screen to their larger bases in Haverfordwest, Pembroke, Carew and Manorbier—they descended on north Pembrokeshire where they built stone castles at Newport and Cilgerran, under the tutelage of marcher lords. They preserved the sanctity of the Celtic shrine of St David by building the great cathedral, and they administered the Welsh province of Dewisland as an ecclesiastical domain. In the whole of north Pembrokeshire they soon came to terms with the Welsh and were absorbed into the local population. In the

south of the county the Welsh never recovered their influence, although the Ordnance Survey map shows the survival of many Celtic place names. In any case Henry I sealed their fate when he introduced the Flemings in the 12th century, probably from somewhere in England where he found them a nuisance. Here they prospered, despite frequent Welsh assaults from the north. They were joined by others. They were good farmers and traders, and they created Little England beyond Wales, that favourite misnomer for the whole county. There is a clear line of demarcation in speech and place names between what are known as the Englishry and the Welshery, or the Landsker line, a word of Norse origin. It runs from Newgale on the coast to Treffgarne where it turns southeast through Narberth to Carmarthen Bay.

The industrial archaeologist will be attracted to the extinct anthracite mining in Freystrop and north of Saundersfoot, the associated iron works at Stepaside; the lime-kilns, particularly those at Tenby, the mills at Carew (tidal) and Blackpool (now a museum), Britain's first ironclad naval vessel, the *Warrior* (now an oil pontoon in Pembroke Dock), Pembroke Dockyard's graving dock and early iron floating tidal gate, the stone-quarrying machinery in ghostly Porthgain on the north coast, the relics of the coastal traffic alongside the quays at Haverfordwest and elsewhere, and the many small harbours.

The architectural achievements are in the castles—Pembroke, Manorbier, Carew—not so grim as the Edwardian fortresses of North Wales. It is worth going a long way to see Carew at high tide, the Keep of Pembroke Castle, and the Gatehouse at Lamphey. Some castles are still inhabited. There are no great houses. Manor houses of Tudor and earlier date have disappeared, or are now farmhouses, having features such as arched doorways and deeply recessed windows influenced by the technique of castle building. One type of farmhouse, peculiar to the county, has a massive exterior chimney, locally called Flemish, the upper stage of which is round and often as much as three feet wide at the top. It is invariably placed at the side of the house, next to the entrance.

p90 'Cock and Hen' entrance gate
Trefasser **(Llanwnda)**
p91 Flemish chimney near **St Davids** ▷

◁ Porthgain **(Llanrian)**
Lime kilns, Kiln Park, **Tenby**

below **Carew** castle

Another feature of this farmhouse is the extension of the ground floor area by recesses roofed over like pent houses, at a flatter slope than that of the main roof. Most of these houses are near St Davids. The cylindrical, bastion-like gateposts at the entrances to churchyards and farms are another— disappearing—feature of the countryside. Usually, each one is topped by a stone, sometimes quartz, sometimes large and smoothed from a nearby beach. The stone on one post, the cock, is traditionally smaller than the other, the hen. They may be a throwback to Viking stockades, the two stones representing the impaled heads of enemies, male and female. There are good examples in the gateways of Bosherston and Robeston West churchyards.

Villages in the north follow the usual Welsh pattern of isolated hamlets. One would expect those in the south to be closer knit, on the English pattern. Sometimes they are, but then the grouping is more aloof than in England. The average village of grey or brownish-grey stucco, with some colour-wash here and there, and some shale or slate building in the north, is undistinguished architecturally, but it has "personality". Here and there, isolated or in rows, will stand outrageously ordinary new houses and bungalows, aggressive with crazy walling, snail pointed, and brightly painted quoins and window surrounds. But the whole will have, somehow, not only a Welsh but a Pembrokeshire character. The landscape absorbs all. But if "development" is carried too far, it will not go on doing so for ever. The county is so blessed in its landscape that it tends to forget it can still be ruined.

Apart from the cathedral at St Davids and the biggish parish churches at Haverfordwest and Tenby, the churches are commonly of two types: the tall-towered churches of Little England, and the towerless, bellcoted churches of the north. The tall towers which usually have a pronounced batter (i.e., they taper upwards), and corbelled-out parapets, were built as refuges, beacons, lookouts, or all three. They are a feature in the south and their drab grey surfaces are often splashed and mottled with white lichen in exposed places, or with rich yellow lichen, moss ferns and penny-royal in the valleys and more sheltered places. Very often the tower is the only part of the church not rebuilt, or much restored. There are two common types of interior, also. The first, usual in the north, has a nave and small chancel, vestry and porch, all Victorianised, white or primrose-yellow washed, with dark-stained furniture and thin, dark rafters. Sometimes there is stained glass in the style of Kempe, or by Celtic Studios; more often the glass is clear, and diamond paned. The church will have been restored or rebuilt in the 1860s or 1870s by one of the architects who became fashionable in these parts, Penson, Lingen Barker, Withers or Dolby. The other type, characteristic of the south, is an irregular rectangle, usually under two gables with a wide, often square, transept or aisle tacked on to enlarge it. Medieval bits—corbels, fonts, arcades, built in crosses—remain in spite of extensive restoration by one of the above. Enormous squints, sometimes amounting to passages, are common. Such a building looks as if it could belong to almost any time between the 12th and 18th centuries, and has of course had alterations at many times. Medieval woodwork (except at St Davids) is rare; later furnishing of interest, such as box pews and unusual liturgical arrangements, rare also. Medieval stained glass is almost non-existent, but there is 18th-century clear glass at Manordeifi and elsewhere. Boxed-in pews, mostly of latish date remain at Bayvil, Loveston, Manordeifi, and Redberth. Sometimes the best building in the village is the Nonconformist Chapel—serviceable, symmetrical and inventive in ornament and decoration, within the strict Classical or Gothic conventions. At the simplest it is a featureless gabled box; at its most elaborate it can be very showy indeed, especially in the north. Some

Bosherston ▷

Baptist chapel, **Solva**

chapels, such as the Congregational Tabernacle in Haverfordwest and the Baptist Hermon in Fishguard glow with colour inside, a foil perhaps to the more sober doctrines preached therein.

The sea is recovering some of the commercial significance of the county of pre-railway days and if oil is found below what is now called the Celtic Sea the effect on the county's economy would be dramatic. Each year more and more people flock to the beaches and caravan camps at the height of

Llangloffan (Granston)

the season. Those who look for solitude and variety will find Pembrokeshire at her uncrowded best between mid-September and mid-July.

Sources of information and other services are:—

(a) The West Wales Naturalists' Trust, which relies on voluntary support to conserve the wild life and natural beauty of West Wales. With the National Parks Committee it has a range of publications for sale, e.g. *The Castles of Pembrokeshire* by Dillwyn Miles, which describes and gives some history of the 15 stone castles in the county as well as listing and locating by Ordnance Survey reference numbers the remains of 34 earthwork castles. Address: 4 Victoria Place, Haverfordwest.

(b) The Pembrokeshire Countryside Unit has information centres at The Norton, Tenby; the County Museum, Haverfordwest; the City Hall, St Davids; the Drill Hall, Pembroke; and at Broad Haven (*see* Walton West in the Gazetteer).

(c) The Field Studies Council has two centres, (*see* Dale and Hundleton in the Gazetteer) for resident students. It is a voluntary organisation, closely associated with Universities and cultural and scientific bodies. Its H.Q. address is 9 Devereux Court, London, W.C.2.

Pattern and texture: ▷
p96 Dyffryn-dwarch, **Granston**
p97 Trefasser (**Llanwnda**)

Pembrokeshire: Gazetteer

The number in brackets refers to the square on the map at the end of the book where the place is to be found.

ABERCYCH [3] Hillside village at *Penrhiw* above junction of Cych and Teifi, once noted for its wood turners. The road up the *Cych Valley* is of a sylvan beauty as far as Pont Cych, where there is a cool pub; then the road climbs out of the valley into bleak moorland.

AMBLESTON [5] Farmhouses and detached cottages, gaily coloured, around the church. This was rebuilt in 1906, except for the plain Norman tower which has a projecting stair turret. Woollen mill at *Wallis*. At nearby *Woodstock* the well-proportioned but rather gloomily grey-washed Methodist chapel (founded 1754, rebuilt 1808) is notable as the first Methodist chapel not consecrated by a bishop in which, in 1755, Holy Communion was celebrated. In a field adjoining *Scollock West Farm* is the 20c monument to yeoman farmers, John and Martha Llewellin. Their life-size, standing effigies are in white marble, detailed to the last gaiter button and dress adornment. Part of the inscription reads "By the blessing of God on their joint undertaking and thrift they bought this farm and hand it down without encumbrance to their heirs. Endeavour to pull together as they did. Union is strength."

AMROTH [9] Seaside village tending to straggle along the

John and Martha Llewellin,
Ambleston

coast road with high shingle banks and at low tide signs of submerged forest. Dominant building, *Amroth Castle*, rebuilt and castellated at end of the 18c, advertises accommodation and caravan park. The church, some way inland on high ground, was enlarged in 1856 by R. K. Penson. Rustic, clumsy arches and plain vaulting typical of the county, and interesting 19c monuments. Best part of parish is the wooded valley bottom west of church, rich with hydrangeas and rhododendrons near tall, end

18c, *Colby Lodge*, designed by John Nash.

ANGLE [8] At sea level at the western end of the county's lower peninsula. The village, a long street of colour-washed cottages is about a mile from the beach at *West Angle Bay*. In the centre the comfortable *Globe Hotel* was converted in 1904 from two houses into a castellated three-storey building and has an open ironwork staircase. Martello tower in village, and *Thorn Island*, once a fort, now a private hotel, are reminders of 19c invasion precautions. Church, thoroughly restored by R. K. Penson in 1850s, has 18c tablets. Behind the church is a miniature fisherman's chapel dedicated to St Anthony. A 1447 foundation, it is raised above a crypt and seats 14 people. It contains a medieval effigy, and modern stained glass at the east end shows Christ walking on the waters. BP tanker terminal in East Bay has offices in a converted fort of 1863 at *Popton Point*. A cannon found in debris has been remounted.

BAYVIL [3] In a circular churchyard, lonely in a field off the Nevern to Cardigan road, a tiny bellcote church with original 19c furniture of simple box pews and pulpit, has recently been rescued from decay. Service once a year.

◁ **Bayvil** church

BEGELLEY [9] The tall church tower used as a lookout in the last war dominates an ugly landscape. The double-aisled church, rough cast and pink-washed inside, was thoroughly restored in 1886; some medieval bits remain. Gipsy camp, now a camp of modern caravans, on *Kings Moor* has associations with Augustus John in his Tenby days. Above on main road, *Zion Calvinist Methodist chapel* (1828, 1866) is neatly square; brown pebble-dash, grey quoins window surrounds and railings.

BLETHERSTON [6] Deeply rural setting; no village, just a tiny church in a tiny churchyard dwarfed by two large adjacent farmsteads. A small bellcote on plain corbels projects from the church's west gable; church is practically square inside with an arcade of three arches. Northern half was Norman but whole renovated in 1880s. Plain, unusual early font has five-sided basin. Kempe-style stained glass in east window.

BONCATH. *See* LLANFIHANGEL PENBEDW.

BOSHERTON [8] Trim, spaced out cottages, a square Georgian house, farm buildings, and a plain cruciform church with strong flavour of medieval stained glass in 1872 three-light window by Clayton and Bell, depicting life of Christ and dedicated to a rector for 41

St Govan's chapel, **Bosherton**

St Govan's Head ▷

years; two female effigies, one hidden by pews. The churchyard cross, probably 14c, has the face of Christ in relief where the arms intersect; the stone of the pillar differs from that of the cross and is probably later. Bosherton Mere is a narrow landlocked inlet famous for pike fishing and its water lilies, the latter at their best in June. If the red flags are not flying you can go through the desolate, treeless, farmless waste created by the M.O.D. Firing Range to the 13c *St Govan's Chapel*, wedged above the sea between two cliffs, at the foot of 50 or so steps and there are more below. There is a superstition that if you count the steps down and then up you never get the same total. The single chamber cell has an earth floor and a natural recess in the rocks behind the altar. Between it and the sea a holy well has been dry for a number of years. There are fine rocks and chasms east and west. *Bullslaughter Bay* and *Flimston Bay*—all difficult of access—and *Huntsman's Leap* are westward. *Broad Haven*, reached by a road down to Trefalen Farm, is an expanse of golden sand, backed by dunes with plenty of shelter eastward underneath the cliffs.

BOULSTON [5] Only the walls remain of the 1843 church on the north bank of the Western Cleddau. There is a right of way through Manor Farm which takes you across ploughland. The alternative is by boat.

BRAWDY [5] The Royal Navy airfield occupies much of this scattered parish at the northern end of St Brides Bay. A recent addition to the airfield is an oceanographic research station, set up by the U.S. Navy and expected to house 250 U.S. sailors by 1975. The 12c bellcote church has been sombrely Victorianized; the floor is well below outside ground level and excessive damp results.

BRIDELL [3] Ogam-inscribed and cross-incised stone, seven feet high, on south side of churchyard. Slate monuments fixed to south wall of simple 1886 church.

BROAD HAVEN. *See* WALTON WEST.

BURTON [8] Mainly populated on the Daugleddau riverside where there is an agreeable country pub; will assume greater importance when a bridge across the water to Pembroke Dock is finished. The church is down a lane a mile or so inland. Its six narrow lancet windows, perhaps 13c, on the south side give it character; the nave and chancel are about 100 years later. 16c altar tomb. Mostly 19c stained glass; bowfronted 19c west gallery with organ. Miniature organ with tiny painted pipes. Eastern side of parish, hardly accessible by car, fronts the Daugleddau estuary; its fine woodlands are best seen from the Lawrenny side.

CALDY ISLAND [9] The motor boat from Tenby harbour takes about half an hour and there is a frequent service in the summer. The island, of 500 acres or so, has had a history of religious communion since Celtic monks founded a monastery, probably in the 6c, and on the site of the old Priory church near the principal source of fresh water. In the 12c the Normans handed the island over to the Benedictine Abbey of St Dogmael in north Pembrokeshire, and monks from there restored the tradition of monastic life by building the Priory church and a monastery adjoining it. They also built St David's church as the parish church of the island. On the suppression of the monasteries in the 16c the monks left. The Priory church was desecrated and a farm was created out of the monastery building. In 1897 the island was bought by the Rev. W. Done Bushell, chaplain of Harrow school, who restored the Priory church to its former use. He also restored St David's church. The east window in the Priory church is a memorial of his work. In 1906 the island was sold to the Benedictine order of monks of the Church of England, who built the present monastery and the Abbey church. In 1913 their Abbot and most of the brothers went over to the Church of Rome. They moved in 1928 to Prinknash Abbey in Gloucestershire and the island was sold to the Cistercians. The Priory, now known as the Old Priory Church, and St David's, are simple pre-Reformation buildings. The *Old Priory* has a leaning spire, cobbled flooring and medieval setting. The richcoloured stained-glass window of St Illtud in the south wall of the nave is by Dom Theodore Baily, a Benedictine. He did other stained glass in *St David's church* and in the cloisters of the monastery. The interior of the Abbey church was gutted by fire in 1940, and restored 10 years later in the Cistercian tradition of austerity, relieved only by the bound choir books on the stalls, and the statue of the Virgin high on the arch behind the High Altar. The monastery buildings were designed in a Romanesque Rhenish style with steep-pitched roofs, turrets and slender pinnacles (Coates Carter, architect). The island is intensively farmed by the monks. Produce is sold on the mainland and in the Caldy Island shop in Tenby. Visitors have unrestricted use of Priory Bay and sands, and restricted access along defined lanes and pathways to the lighthouse, built in 1828, the three churches and the village around the monastery. The village houses a small community of lay residents whose number increases from about forty in the winter to a hundred or so in the summer.

CAMROSE [5] The principal feature of this otherwise flat parish, the home of the newspaper Berry family, is *Dudwell Mountain* an expanse of grass, gorse, and forestry plantations; it rises about 400 feet above the rest of the parish, which is cut into sections by fast roads to the west and north coasts. The village is an angular pattern of cottages, rectory and church, the latter promising well outside with its five-sided turret to the tower and painted weathercock, but barnlike and featureless inside. Round "Flemish" chimney in a farm yard at Dudwell end of lane from church.

CAPEL COLMAN [3] *Cilwendeg*, now an old people's home, is a large mansion in spreading parkland with well-disposed plantations overlooking the Dulas valley. Its oldest part, Classical, is of about 1830 and was obscured later in the 19c by a porte cochère in biscuit-coloured stone on the north side, by an addition in similar stone with fluted pilasters on the south side, and by conservatory extensions. There is a courtyard of attractive old stables and kennels, behind double bowfronts divided by an open archway. Remains of an early 19c grotto with shell-lined walls and intricate flooring in the shrubbery. Square, twin, single-storey lodges at one entrance to the park and a pair of two-storey lodges at another. Across the park at the end of a lane, the solitary church (architect Daniel Davies) was rebuilt in 1835 and lightly restored in 1900. From the outside it looks like a toytown fort with its pinnacled slender tower and porch; it is all of slate and very rustic in design. Inside it is a small rectangular chamber with a pine panelled west gallery on pine columns, diamond-paned tinted glass and flat plastered ceiling. 18c tablets by Lewis, Cheltenham, and two medallions. Yew trees and view of Preseli hills.

CAREW [9] The castle rises, at high tide like a mirage, above a creek of the Carew river. It is privately owned and open to the public. Some Norman military architecture of the 13c includes massive circular towers. The 15c Great Hall was built by Sir Rhys ap Thomas between the two west towers, and the unfinished Elizabethan state-rooms on the north side with their huge mullioned windows were added by Sir John Perrot. They mark the transition from military to domestic. The nearby three-storey *French Mill* (traditionally so-called because when the Mill was built in the 16c the stones came from France), one of the few surviving tide-mills in the U.K., stopped working as a mill in 1880, and silting left it derelict between the castle and the entrance to the creek. Restoration by the owners, the trustees of Anthony Trollope-Bellew, aided by outside bodies has been ingeniously carried out to the tidal flood gates, the mill-wheel sluices, the river dam, and the mill machinery. The tide flows into a big pond which half surrounds the castle and out under a causeway. The speed in which the owners are putting the mill on view and the accruing educational value justified the judges in awarding third place in the second (1972) series of awards by the Royal Institute of Chartered Surveyors.

Near the castle entrance stands the early 11c *Carew Cross*. Slightly over 13 feet high, an inscription shows it to be a royal memorial to Maredudd ap Edwin who ruled south-west Wales early in the 11c. It is the largest, most elaborately carved, and best-preserved of the three Pembrokeshire sculptured crosses, and is closely related in style to the one in Nevern churchyard. The carving on each of the four faces of the shaft of interlacing patterns of fret and strap work, ·scrolls, and looped vine tendrils reflects Celtic and Northumbrian influ-

ence. Below the Carew Arms Inn a Wesleyan (1852) Chapel is of original design. Near the side of the road and behind the Inn a "Flemish" chimney stands curiously detached. Southward across the main road, the church tower and its corner steeple can be seen from a distance. Restorers have been careful with this spacious 15c church and tombs and effigies of crusaders. A stone-flagged floor (except where the front pews have recently been removed and the floorspace filled with concrete slabs) and medieval tiles give it character, which cemented walls, ceiling and "cathedral" glass dilute. The *Old Rectory*, 100 yards west, has a square corbelled 16c tower and an arched doorway. It has recently been restored.

This large parish extends north to the Cresswell river taking in Cresswell Quay and Williamston West. *Cresswell Quay* has a good creeper-clad pub, and plenty of atmosphere, to be seen preferably at high tide. There are stone quarries still at *Williamston West*; 80 years ago they employed 150 men and the stone was taken down by barge on the tide to Milford Haven. It was also used for building the Pembroke Dockyard. The village is little more than the nucleus of two substantial farms with some modernised cottages. An 1844 simple, single-chamber church in classical style is now a piggery and one senses the loss of the three pubs which used to be in this Sleeping Beauty of a village which might have been transplanted from deepest Oxfordshire.

CASTLEBYTHE. *See* PUNCHESTON.

CASTLEMARTIN [8] The round-about in the middle of the village, which gave its name to a breed of long-horned black cattle, was once the pound. Most of the parish has been de-populated and its farms and country houses demolished since it became a Royal Armoured Corps firing range. When the red flags are flying, gunfire is unceasing. The church down a side road is worth a visit. The yard gates are 1890 cast iron with texts worked in. The church inside has details including an arcade of pointed Early English arches of mottled mountain limestone which look well against the white walls. The font is Norman. A tablet says that the 1842 organ belonged to Mendelssohn and came here via Sibton, Suffolk. The floor rises steeply east-wards. Outside, up the bank that encourages this rise and against the east side of the churchyard, are the tangled ruins of a roofless building known as the "*Old Rectory*". In it are low archways, a circular pier and a capital with carved faces.

CILGERRAN [3] This large vil-lage is characteristically Welsh in style and layout, more like those of neighbouring Car-diganshire; the older houses built largely of slate slabs from the local quarries, now too deep for economical working. All that remains of the *Norman Castle* are the two circular towers, of this slate, defending the inner ward. The site was given to the National Trust by Mrs Colby of Ffynnone. The sheer view from the castle into the Teifi gorge is awesome;

Richard Wilson painted it, so did J. M. W. Turner. The cupola of *Coedmore House* peep-ing through the trees on the opposite bank adds a touch of South Kensington. The church, above a hollow and a cluster of gaily-painted cottages, is large and, except for the 13c tower, mid-19c. All the windows now have stained glass; two (by Cel-tic Studios) have lower panels of farm scenes, tractors, etc, and of coracles in the Teifi below the castle. There are popular coracle races in August. *1862 Baptist Chapel, Penuel*, is classi-cal, with long windows. Showy, with pale-grey and apricot coat.

CILRHEDYN WEST [2] The road from the Cych valley enters the uplands here; sad 1853 church with texts in Greek and Hebrew in the porch.

CLARBESTON [5] Deeply set in featureless rusticity above the Syfni valley. Battlemented, towered church looks better from a distance; interior is run-of-the-mill Victorian. Solid, square, stone-built farmhouse neighbours it. At *Clarbeston Road*, three miles away, where the railway forks, quite an attractive and lively village has grown up.

CLYDAI [3] Sparse upland country with sudden valleys, the best at *Star* where the battle-mented tower and high spire of the church are on the hillside; restored north aisle arcade has compressed the chancel; rood loft steps, stone flags and pointed arches in 13c tower. Three incised stones have been taken into the church. The road through Bwlch y groes and Star can be used as a direct road between Carmarthen and the coast around Newport.

Tegryn is a rather grim cross-roads hamlet from which a narrow road drops sharply past massive Congregational chapel (1805 to 1874) at *Llwynyrhwrdd* with a gradient of one in four into the next valley.

COSHESTON [8] At *Jenkins Point* to the north of the parish, the Cleddau, Carew, and Cresswell rivers meet on their seaward way to Milford Haven. A peaceful place, now reflecting, like Lawrenny on the other side of the Cresswell river, the growing enthusiasm for sailing. The view of yachts in the water at high tide is enhanced by *Benton Castle* in the trees on the other bank, a miniature Schloss, built by the Normans about 1300 to overlook the junction. It is now a private house, adapted from 1932 onwards. The village is much on the English nucleus pattern, tidy and gay with colour wash. Village pub has a low, early Victorian front, concealing earlier building. The church was almost rebuilt in 1855; its best feature is the slender tower and octagonal steeple carrying a vane dated 1781.

CRESSWELL   QUAY.   *See* CAREW.

CRINOW [6] Tiny parish includes Narberth railway station, a country house or two and *Clynpattel* Norman motte castle. A simple bellcote church is hidden by yews, high laurels and other evergreens.

CRUNWEAR [8] A south-sloping site backed by the wooded hills towards Tavernspite. A track through the fields takes you to the churchyard, and a cobbled path to the isolated church, rebuilt in 1843 except for the tall three-storeyed tower. It was restored in 1878 (architect T. David, Laugharne). It has high arches to both transepts, a modern rood across the chancel arch, clear white walls, and plenty of light through clear-glass lattice windows.

CRYMMYCH [3] The southern half is in Llanfyrnach parish, the northern in Llanfair Nant Gwyn. Old and new highways converge here, the prehistoric ridgeway over the Preseli hills towards St Davids, the Cardigan to Tenby main road and the dead railway from Whitland to Cardigan. The village which grew out of the railway is still raw, with a thriving trade in agricultural machinery and services. What from a distance looks like an airport control tower turns out to be a modern school in glass and yellow brick, its campus the Preseli range.

DALE [7] Attractive estuary village with a view of part of Milford Haven's new development in the distance across the water. It has the sea on three rocky, or mudflat, sides. Once a flourishing seaport, now in the summer a flourishing yachting centre, with quayside pub. Nothing of interest in the small, towered church and the castle is mainly modern, and a residence. The village is sheltered by bowed, blown trees and up a steep hill on the tip of Dale

Point is the Victorian Fort. It houses the *Dale Fort Field Centre* of the Field Studies Council. It is open each year from end of February to beginning of November and can take up to fifty residential students wishing to study some branch of science or fine art; most commonly studied are branches of Natural History (*see* Introduction).

On the map the road to *St Ann's Head* looks more interesting than it is; it ends at the gates of the coastguard station and lighthouse. Below, *Cobblers Hole* displays magnificent geological folds in the Devonian rocks. Dale is said to have more sunshine than any other Welsh place, and is noted for early crops.

DINAS [2] One of the best, middle-distance prospects of landscape in the county is from the crest of the *Gelli* hill out of Fishguard; it is one of gorse, bracken, and rock outcrops as the land rises into the foothills of *Dinas Mountain*, and of small, stone-walled fields and low whitewashed farms. You might be anywhere on the Brittany or north Spanish coast. The road dips into the village to a narrow defile below what seems to be a miniature Iron Age fort of loose stones on a hillock. The village straggles along the main coast road to its council house outskirts; there are two other settlements, one at *Brynhenllan* with a hamlet community on the way down to the dark beach at *Pwllgwaelod* and the *Sailors Safety* inn, the other at *Cwmyreglwys*, once a thriving fishing village, now almost entirely summer-residential,   with   caravans.

The Teifi at **Cilgerran**

Between the two beaches the farm of toad shaped *Dinas Island* (scene of R. M. Lockley's *Island Farmers*) rises seaward and is separated from the mainland by a narrow marsh. There have been two churches in Dinas before the present one, built in 1861 (architect R. K. Penson) at a cost of about £900, by two village brothers barely out of their teens; one at *Brynhenllan Farm*, destroyed by the Vikings; the other built at sea level at Cwmyreglwys, and overthrown in the great storm of October 1859 in which the *Royal Charter* went down off Anglesey. Of this only the west wall remains with

its low pointed arch. The central churchyard, now protected by a wall from the sea, keeps this picturesque bay inviolate from further "development". Two chapels, dark grey *Brynhenllan* (Methodist 1799) and *Gideon* (Congregational 1830), have the simple dignity of earlier nonconformist architecture. The round-headed surrounds to the square sash windows, the striking name lozenge on the gabled front and the scrolled iron gates give Baptist (1792) *Tabor* a faintly baroque air. It is undoubtedly the most distinguished building in the village. The church and chapel

burial grounds attest, in their tombstone inscriptions, to the importance of the village as a nursery of deep-sea sailors. Seals breed in the caves below Dinas Island, and on it within living memory a special breed of large horned goats roamed. Buzzards and ravens nest in the cliffs, as well as innumerable sea birds. There is excellent walking on Dinas Mountain, as there is, too, on the coastal path round Dinas Island.

EGLWYSWRW [3] The church, virtually rebuilt in 1883 (architects Middleton and Son, Cheltenham), dominates the village.

Abergwaun (Lower Fishguard)

The site is circular, which suggests that it is ancient, pre-Christian, as no doubt are numerous upright boulders in walls, and in use as gateposts. Sergeant's Inn on the main road takes its name either from quartering of troops at the time of the French invasion (*see* Llanwnda) or, more probably, from advocates attending sessions in the tiny adjacent courtroom.

FISHGUARD [2] Friendly, intimate town; the hub is the market place. The Market Hall (also local authority offices) is a neat, classical, mid-19c building. On the other side, a sign over the door of the chocolate-coloured 'Royal Oak' says that, within, the last invasion of Britain ended with the signing of surrender terms (*see* Llanwnda). The Cardigan road

drops steeply to sea level at *Lower Fishguard* past a tall warehouse, once connected with the herring industry and now the Sea Scouts' quarters. This picturesque setting of quayside, bridge over the Gwaun river, and cottage rows was chosen for a recent *Under Milk Wood* film. Up the Gwaun valley from the bridge a track leads to *Plas Glynamel*, now a guest-house. It was

built in 1800 by Richard Fenton, author of *A Historical Tour through Pembrokeshire* and friend of Oliver Goldsmith, Sir Joshua Reynolds, Edmund Burke and Dr Johnson. Much of what he wrote about is now in ruins or has disappeared. Some of the blame must go to him, for he attacked dolmen and tumulus with the eager vigour of the 18c amateur archaeologist. His wife was French, and it is thought that Plas Glynamel, a plain Classical façade, with raised steps on either side of the front entrance was suggested by a French house. During the American War of Independence, Fishguard had a visit from the sea raider, Paul Jones, who put an armed party ashore at Lower Fishguard, demanding 500 guineas. To hurry things forward he fired two broadsides, one of which maimed Fenton's sister, Mary, for life. The ransom was then paid.

Nonconformist chapel architecture is best represented by central Baptist Hermon (1776 and 1832). Façade is classical, almost top heavy with portico and pediment. The interior, well lit naturally through clear glass on two levels, has a gallery on four sides, three panelled in wood, the fourth in open-pattern painted ironwork. Grained box pews and decorated plaster ceiling—all very showy and not at all in the minor key which one associates with religious dissent. The Parish Church, 1857, is small beer beside it. The 1918 Roman Catholic church on the way to the harbour is light and simple; two stained-glass windows, the lancet by Harry Clarke of Dublin and the one at the east end by Dom Theodore Baily, O.S.B. (see Caldy Island). The Irish connexion is very evident and Irish coinage is interchangeable with English. (See also Goodwick.)

FRESHWATER EAST [8] Utterly abandoned to caravans, chalets and facilities. In Lamphey civil parish.

FRESHWATER WEST [8] Partly in Angle, partly in Castlemartin civil parishes, a four-mile stretch of sand and low rocks, over which the Atlantic rollers sweep. Quicksands, and very dangerous bathing. Near the point where a narrow bridge crosses the main road at sea level, the water coming from Castlemartin is piped to the sea through a curious tunnel of wood slats. 1914–1918 War Memorial Calvary at the northern end of the bay, the watchtowers and red flags of the Royal Armoured Corps Firing Range at the other. Desolate dunes, known locally as burrows, stretch far inland, rising as high as 200 feet towards the reclaimed and fertile valley north of Castlemartin village. The *Devils Quoit Dolmen* is about

130 paces over the low fence opposite the drive entrance to Broomhill Farm on the Angle road. About three feet above the ground, the enormous capstone, supported on two uprights on one side, has collapsed on the third.

FREYSTROP [5] A straggling village, mainly of new houses and bungalows along the Haverfordwest to Burton road. A lane signposted "Freystrop church and Little Milford" takes you steeply through woods and past a nursery of young trees to the edge of the tidal river, but there is little room for manœuvre at the end. The simple bellcote church was practically rebuilt in its attractive setting in 1874 (architect E. H. Lingen Barker). It has a Norman font, and a 1762 tablet to the untimely death of Caesar Mathias, ending:

Thou'rt not too young tho' at the
  age of seven
T'enjoy thy God and reign an
  Heir of Heaven.

FURZY PARK AND PORTFIELD [5] A civil parish with no centre of settlement, through which traffic hurries eagerly to and from Haverfordwest and Broad Haven.

GOODWICK [2] Early in this century the village of fishermen's cottages on the shore of Fishguard bay had high hopes of becoming a terminal for the Atlantic liner traffic. So part of the cliff face was torn down to make Fishguard Harbour, the Victorian Wyncliffe house extended to become the Great Western Railway's *Bay Hotel*,

and terraced houses added to the hillside slopes. But disappointment came and the terminal is now confined to traffic with southern Irish ports. The foundation stone of a fine upstanding parish church was laid in 1910 and Colonel Bruce Vaughan's design allowed for extension beyond the west wall, which is still disconcertingly blank. Otherwise the church is a fine one of its period. The barrel roof has gilded bosses and chairs in place of pews. There are only two stained-glass windows, both in the chancel, that at the east end by Christopher Powell, of Highgate. In the arch of the doorway behind the altar in the south aisle chapel is an Annunciation by Stanley Lewis, Carmarthen, showing Fishguard Bay and Dinas Head in the background.

GRANSTON [5] *Tregwynt*, the principal house of this small parish has a plain Georgian front; picturesque out-buildings follow the curve of the road at the entrance drive. It stands high, overlooking the valley through which a small stream flows from the marshy ground in the north to join the sea at *Aberbach*, a secluded private beach of Treseissyllt farm. Seissyllt (Cecil is the English variant) is an old Welsh family name. Inside Tregwynt there was the sound of revelry by night when news of the imminent French invasion (*see* Llanwnda) struck like a rising knell on the ears of the county's Beauty and Chivalry, gathered there at a ball. The woollen mill in the valley below Tregwynt, once water but now machine driven, attracts many visitors.

112

belong to the landscape. Here we see Wales as it looked 150 years ago. Old ways and traditions linger among the people, who still celebrate New Year's Day on January 13th, according to the old calendar. In the morning the children sing from house to house while their parents prepare for the night celebrations, when the old tradition of the open house is preserved by some. There are four churches in the valley, Llanychaer, Llanychllwydog, Pont Faen and Cilgwyn. *Llanychaer*, rebuilt 1871 (architect E. Dolby) and *Cilgwyn*, rebuilt 1883 (architect E. Lingen Barker), are of no interest nor is the interior of *Llanychllwydog*, rebuilt 1860 (architect R. J. Withers), where there are four stones incised with Celtic crosses in the churchyard. *Pont Faen* church was practically rebuilt from a ruin in the 1860s and has later been richly embellished by the Ardern family, some of whose ashes are preserved in caskets in a grilled niche in the chancel wall. The vestments include four embroidered copes. The Arderns lived in the old house which has been considerably modernised, and is now divided into two, opposite the church. *Kilkiffeth*, now a farmhouse remote on the moor above Pont Faen, has outside features, such as a low, stone-vaulted passage, blocked at one end, and traces of a large walled garden, to account for Fenton's mention of it in his *Tour through Pembrokeshire* as "the seat of the monarchs of our mountain squires". The kitchen of the

Bench end detail, St Mary's, **Haverfordwest**

now modernised, plain farm-house is heavily raftered and a small block of Cotswold-type stone with linear carving has found its way, from some grander building, among the rough outside stones.

HAROLDSTON ST ISSELLS [5] Simple 19c bellcote church on the right bank of the Western Cleddau, past Lower Harold-ston farm near Merlins Bridge. *Haroldston*, now in ruins, was the birthplace of Elizabethan Sir John Perrott (*see* Carew).

HAROLDSTON WEST [5] A high windswept parish above St Bride's Bay. Dull 1870 church.

HASGUARD [7] One of the few buildings in this rustic parish is the primitive double bellcote church; it has a narrow, stone-flagged, medieval nave from which a low arch opens into a modern chancel. Finely-weathered exterior of grey and red sandstone and latticed win-dows. From the churchyard you can hear the whistles of ships in the Haven.

HAVERFORDWEST [5] The county town, not only rich in charters and ancient privileges but unique in West Wales for variety and visual interest, and best seen on foot. Much has been done and is being done to clear the untidiness at river level where the Western Cled-dau runs parallel to A40 under two bridges (the older one on the north side built in 1726), downstream past crumbling warehouses on the quayside and the *Bristol Trader*, the latter an eponymous reminder of the town's seaport days. On the left

bank of the river the new local authority offices, Cambria House, and a new coach-station occupy much of the recently cleared land. The outside of Cambria House (architects A. Geens and Max Cross) is ribbed concrete with panels of Llan-golman slates, which are also used for the groundfloor in-side.

Main roads over the bridges carry west coast traffic up the steep medieval streets. Build-ings to catch the eye up the High Street as far as St Mary's church are, first, the *Masonic Hall* (1872), in Picton Place; its Corinthian portico and pedi-ment were almost certainly designed by G. Morgan of Car-marthen; then, almost oppo-site, the plain well-pro-portioned Georgian front of the *Castle Hotel*; As the street rises the *Shire Hall* is an eye-catcher with its Ionic Greek Revival façade. Inside, in the main courtroom, it has an arcade of Ionic columns, and coats of arms. Tall houses, some three-storeyed, with plain Georgian fronts above the shop levels, continue the rising street line. *St Mary's Church* gives an imme-diate impression of austere spa-ciousness as the light through clear-glass windows falls across the north aisle and through the splendid 13c arcade of pointed arches. The pews are well-spaced and the floor, except for the red-tiled chancel, has a bold pattern of cream freestone and slate. The late Perpendicular clerestory gives height, and the very fine flat oak roof is Tudor. The 19c stained glass in the east window is better than average, and a casque and crest of the Phillips family of Picton Castle,

mounted high on the north wall, add panache. The Mayor and Sheriff's pew has an ela-borately carved 14c bench-end. On the raised west end platform there is a mutilated effigy of a pilgrim to Compostella, and a long 1734 beam on which the names of rector and churchwar-dens are carved. A hatchment of the Phillips family hangs on the south wall. Market Street, branching left from the church, climbs higher still into St Thomas' parish which contains the Council Offices and hos-pital, and an enormous fair-ground-like open space bordered by old town houses, which are also in evidence in a parallel street. *St Thomas' church*, other than its tall plain 13c tower, was wholly rebuilt in the mid 19c and is dull. *Goat Street* runs down hill from Market Street and contains many of the old town houses of the county gentry, notably *Foley House* once the town house of the Foleys of Ridgeway in Llawhaden. Designed by John Nash, it is now (1973) the committee-room centre for the County Council. Its street elevation is marred by a rough textured coating, and it is best seen from the garden below its eastern ele-vation. Inside, it has the typical Nash S-shaped iron staircase balusters. Farther down, *Her-mon Hill House* has a pretty bow front.

The *Norman Castle* and the old gaol beside it, above the north bridge, impress from a distance

117

but the castle was roughly treated in the Civil War. The prison has become the new *County Museum* which has an excellent display of county relics and modern art. *Dark Street* running from St Mary's to the boldly black-and-white painted *Mariners Hotel* has a line of warehouses on one side with tall, blocked, arched entrances, the whole rather like a fragment of an Italian hill town. In *Barn Street* the faded azure blue, winged bow front of 1774 *Tabernacle*, a house with intricate cast ironwork, and *Bethesda Baptist Chapel* (1878, Welsh Romanesque) are worth looking for. The Tabernacle has elaborate colour decoration inside and the ceiling plaster work is said to be by Italian craftsmen. It should be seen by anyone interested in chapel architecture (the key is at 67 City Road round the corner). *St Martins church* nearby has a distinctive tower and stone spire. It is 100 years older than St Mary's and the south chapel was added in the 14c. Lofty and uncluttered, it has five steps from the nave up to the chancel and sanctuary. The adjacent *Wesleyan chapel* was an adjunct of St Martins before the 1811 rift with the Established Church. West Wales Gliding Club headquarters are at *Withybush Aerodrome* on the Fishguard road.

HAYSCASTLE [5] The low medieval church, beautifully weathered and simply restored, is a good neighbour to the splendid old farmhouse and buildings beside it. From it a rushy valley carries the eye seaward across Brandy Brook, the western boundary of the parish.

HENRY'S MOAT [5] A farm or two and a Victorian nave and chancel church with a bellcote, on the edge of a steep declivity. The nearby Motte from which its name has come is a Norman castle mound, deep in bracken and brambles and encompassed by a fairly wide ditch.

HERBRANDSTON [8] On the north bank of Milford Haven, and the site of two oil refineries. The village is a group of houses and single-storey cottages around a green. Among the elms on one side, the church of grey and red sand-stone looks well with its low square and slate-roofed tower. Inside it has been refurnished in oak, and corbel stones sculpted in the form of human heads are the only medieval features. The chancel walls are of unplastered, mottled red sandstone.

HODGESTON [8] The grouped village is surrounded by open, well-farmed country. The church has 14c decorated work, and is plain, open, and undisturbed by restoration or ill-directed piety.

HOOK. *See* LLANGWM.

HUBBERSTON [8] This hamlet is now submerged in the urban development of Milford. The tiny, tall-towered church has a 14c stone sedilia.

HUNDLETON [8] *Orielton*, built in 1743 on an older foundation for the Owen family which came from Anglesey, is the principal house and estate. By west Wales standards it is impressive. The urns have recently been

taken down from each corner of the plain classical east front but the south front is more elaborate, and the Owen arms, painted on the rainwater downspouts, add colour to the stone face. Inside there is a stone staircase with iron balustrade. It is now a Field Centre of the Field Studies Council. About 2,000 students pass through it each year; their main fields of study are geography and marine biology. The road from Pembroke takes you through a shady valley to the sparse village. The 1933 roadside church is a low brick building with a red pantile roof (architect Ellery Anderson, Cheltenham).

JEFFRESTON [9] A hilltop cluster of houses crowned by a tall-towered Victorianised church. The churchyard is circular, which suggests a pre-Christian site. Solidly built houses are coated with stucco and pebbledash. *Cresselly* is a 1777 stone Georgian house on an earlier site. In Fenton's day it was in the centre of the anthracite mines which have long since disappeared. The house was screened from them by plantations. There is now talk of opencast mining hereabouts.

JOHNSTON [5] Growing influence of the new Milford Haven. Sprawl and untidiness. New council houses on main road. Church, 13c and later, has tall, battered tower and squints on either side of chancel arch. Careful 1909 restoration. From the church gates you can see, framed in a wrought-iron gateway, the low two-storeyed south front of *Johnston Hall*, once the seat of the Kensington family from which the London area takes its name. The Hall has been altered and has early-Victorian bay windows on the south front.

JORDANSTON [5] Last-but-one station on the Paddington–Fishguard run. Church and farm make a group under a rookery. *Jordanston Hall* (the farm) is large, 17c and now split up. Church, rebuilt in 1797, restored with the addition of a tower in 1863. East window by Celtic Studios. The Hamilton family (*see* Milford) owned much land hereabouts and their hatchment hangs on the west wall flanked by the Lord's Prayer and the Creed engraved on slate slabs. 17c tablets. Early-17c tombstone in chancel. Grey plaster walls. *Llangwarren* is a demure, stone-built house of the squirearchy, enlarged in the 18c. There are traces of the small earlier farmhouse. It adorns its southern aspect across a valley with plantations and the grounds in the spring are yellow with daffodils. An inscribed stone of the Dark Ages, (5 to 7c) stands in the grounds.

LAMBSTON [5] Still a deeply rural parish although coming under the influence of expanding Haverfordwest. The small bellcote church, medieval and restored in 1890 has weathered to a pleasant grey and goes well with the farm buildings near it. Circular churchyard suggests a pre-Christian site.

LAMPETER (or LLANBEDR) VELFREY [6] Small village on either side of a winding road down to the bellcote church

among yews, in a raised and circular churchyard. Inside, an arcade of five Early English arches separates south aisle from nave, and there is a 17c altar tomb in the south-east corner; some early 20c stained glass. Six roads converge on the county boundary at *Tavernspite*, "Spite" being a corruption of Welsh *yspytty*, hospice.

LAMPHEY [8] Tightly knit village of tiny railway station, houses old and new, and church; the latter was modernised in the 19c and the tower and font are all that is left of the original Norman foundation. There is a "Flemish" chimney, free-standing like the one at Carew, in a garden on a housing estate. *Lamphey Court* lies in a Jane Austen setting across the fields and the Bishop's Palace is nearby. The Court is outwardly the best preserved house in the Classical Revival style of the 1820s in the county. It has a tall Ionic portico, pedimented, as a central feature of the south front, and is built of warm, yellow stone. Two and a half acres of the Court's estate are now (1973) under vines; it is expected that within the next year or so the experiment will be advanced enough to yield a marketable wine of the Hock type from Riesling and Sylvaner vines. If successful, more vines will be planted.

The *Bishop's Palace*, now the property of the Department of the Environment, is an extensive and handsome ruin (14 to 16c) in grey and sepia stone, freckled with white lichen. The detached gatehouse in the centre of the enclosure is as sufficient and harmonious a

structure as a North African Marabout shrine, and the vaulted undercroft of the hall is a dramatic area with natural lighting filtering from each side. What Gandolpho is to the Vatican, Lamphey was to St Davids. To this quiet place with its deer park, fish ponds, mills and orchards the bishops of St Davids retired for leisure, and two of them in particular have left their mark, Bishop Gower (1327–47) in his Great Hall, so like his Cathedral Palace, and Bishop Vaughan (1509–23), employing the same Cotswold stone in the Chapel as he used in St Davids. At the Reformation the Palace passed into the Devereux family and Robert, Earl of Essex, Elizabeth's favourite, spent his boyhood here. The place is far less beautiful than it was before the Department of the Environment (then Commissioner of Works) took it over in 1957. It was then highly picturesque but now has been given, too thoroughly and clinically for many tastes—dare we say it—the Works.

LAWRENNY [8] Out of season a placid, backwater village of cottages, grouped in the shadow of the church at the entrance to Lawrenny Hall, now demolished. Monuments in church. The road to the left bank of the Daugleddau is lined with oak trees twisted and torn by gales, Rackhamesque but beautiful. The ferry no longer plies but within recent years a one-time small caravan park has become an active yachting and sailing base. There is a club house, and chalets in the background.

121

Lamphey Bishop's Palace

LETERSTON [5] On A40. Once
an important north Pembrokeshire cattle market. Bungalows
and refaced houses belie its antiquity. 1881 church (architect
Lingen Barker) has simple interior with heraldic cross,
medieval piscina and female
effigy. Saron Baptist chapel
(1828, 1869) has good windows
and doorway in stone-faced
gable end.

LITTLE NEWCASTLE [5] A
grass-grown mound, the site of
a Norman castle, around which
the village of houses and single-
storey cottages has haphazardly
grown. On one side stands the

simple, bellcote church of 1870.
Birthplace of renowned early
18c pirate, Bartholomew
Roberts (Black Barti).

LLANBEDR VELFREY. *See*
LAMPETER VELFREY.

LLANDEWI VELFREY [6] The
foursquare Baptist Chapel on
A40 going towards Haver-
fordwest, about a mile west of
the post office catches the eye,
but not so quickly as it did when
it was painted stark white; it is
now grey. A gallery pillar, inside, is dated 1832 but the outside looks older. It has a good
gallery. Opposite the doorway

the tombstone of Evan Thomas
of Panteg (d. 1871) has an inscription in Bardic Script. The
parish church is hidden in lanes
overlooking Marlais valley.
Rebuilt 100 years or so ago it
lacks interest except for a Norman corbel stone on which two
heads are carved one above
the other. The top one has a
long down-turned, protruding
tongue, Aztec like.

LLANDEILO [6] A narrow strip
next to Maenclochog. Ruins of
St Teilo's church barely discer-
nible in Llandeilo Farm. *Temple
Druid* on the Llangolman road,
in a beautiful valley and park-

land setting of beech and chestnut, is an interesting house. Remoter history tells of its being a hunting lodge; an 1821 sale catalogue attributes it to John Nash. It might well be by him. It is a simple two-storeyed house with wide eaves, a horizontal band halfway up, and a pillar on each side of the doorway. An alcove entrance from the hall to the drawing-room flanked by curved doors suggests Nash. There is a similar feature on a finer scale in his house at Ffynnone. The house has been remodelled on an earlier building. The inside walls are massive and the cellar has a stone vaulted roof. There is a Congregational chapel, also on this road, in pale grey-washed slate blocks, mainly of 1845, with 1882 and 1931 renovations.

LLANDELOY [5] The countryside and village are dull, but the tiny church, rebuilt in 1924 (by J. Coates Carter, of Prestbury, Glos.) has re-created the features of an early Celtic church on a three-level plan, squint, rood loft and all. The interior would look less artificial, and be lighter, if the rough masonry could be lightly plastered and painted white.

LLANDISSILIO WEST [6] Dull nave-and-chancel church, off the main road, in a straggling, dark-brown and grey village.

LLANFAIR NANT Y GOF [5] Church is a simple well-designed (possibly by R. J. Withers) 1855 rebuilding, overlooking a valley which the Admiralty Depot of Trecwn disfigures.

Lamphey Bishop's Palace gatehouse

LLANFAIR NANT GWYN [3] *Pantyderi*, now a guest-house, is a well-sited early 17c house with mid-19c additions, and a view of the Preselis. The church was rebuilt (architect R. J. Withers) in 1855. It has an elegant spire over the west gable.

LLANFALLTEG WEST [6] Lovely south-facing site with the feeling of being miles from anywhere—as indeed it is. Little more than a church and tree-shaded farm, looking across to climbing meadows. Victorian dullness of the church is mildly assuaged by pink colouring, and scroll over chancel arch: *One faith, one Lord, one baptism.*

LLANFIHANGEL PENBEDW [3] The church, practically rebuilt in 1859 (architect R. J. Withers), is long and low, standing forlornly in an acre of empty churchyard. With its squat west tower and weathered stone it looks well from the outside but is plain and rudimentary inside. *Cilrue*, nearby, now a farm, has a drive winding down an avenue of beech trees to a large circular fish-pond opposite the front door. The house is pre-Georgian; it has a broad Jacobean staircase and

123

panelling in downstairs rooms. Main centre of population is *Boncath*, a cross-roads cluster of grey, 18c and earlier houses, grown with the arrival of the railway into a small village. Boncath is Welsh for buzzard, a fairly common sight in these parts.

LLANFYRNACH [6] A largish village in a valley on the dead line from Whitland to Cardigan. The lead mines up the valley are also dead and so are the large slate quarries at *Glogue*. Despite this, the village has a cheerful look with plenty of colour and fresh paint. The slaty church has a medieval tower, otherwise it is very dull. There is a disused railway halt at Glogue and a row of houses facing the line. *Hermon* is a typically Welsh haphazard cluster of houses along a main road. Down the Taf valley, *Glandwr* is a substantial hamlet. Its Congregational chapel (1712, 1717, 1774, 1836, 1876) has a good façade in deep cream

with apricot quoins and drip courses. Inside are two good memorials, one to Lazarus Howel "who entered his disembodied state Jan. 15th 1776" and the other to John Devonald who gave the land on which the chapel stands. Both are in English, surprisingly, since English is rarely heard here. Splendid colour inside, and fine semi-circular sweep of pews and gallery.

LLANGAN WEST [6] Sad Victorian church in the middle of nowhere, north of Whitland.

LLANGOLMAN [6] Forlorn Victorian bellcote church on hillside. The slate quarries are still being worked. One of the buildings roofed with slates quarried here is the Natural History Museum in South Kensington.

LLANGWM [5] Once the centre of the Milford Haven oyster fishery but now down to cockles. A large village, the inhabitants of which are stated by some to

Lamphey Court ▷
(vineyard beyond)

be Flemish in origin and by others a Norse remnant. They have a reputation for sturdy independence. The houses are attractively spaced out overlooking a valley near the Cleddau rivers. The small bellcote church has good light from clear-glass windows on to white walls. The canopied niche tombs with effigies of a knight and wife are partly hidden. A piscina is decorated with shields and finial, borne on a circular shaft. Benefaction board. View of estuary, trees and distant Picton Castle and parkland at *Black Tar Point*, where you can dig for cockles in the mud. Up the Western Cleddau is the village of *Hook* where an ancient colour-washed cottages with trim square windows blend with modern development. Hook was important locally as a mining area for the best anthracite in the country. The mines closed in 1948, as they did

Lamphey Bishop's Palace

Abereiddy, **Llanrian**

not fit into the Coal Board pattern. From the road you see no trace of them, nor of the narrow gauge track which took the tubs to a jetty where much of the coal was loaded into French ships.

LLANHOWELL [4] *Carn Treglemais*, a natural outcrop, rises high above the windswept plain. The L-shaped farmhouse on the roadside north of the Carn is a splendid example of the solid, slurry-roofed houses

along the north Pembrokeshire coast. Medieval church on the hill going down into the Solva valley has Celtic simplicity. Much restored; but its irregular shape is pleasing.

LLANLLAWER [2] If stones and boulders give you any sensual link with the far off past, this is the parish for you. Marked *Trellan* on the O.S. maps, it lies on a ridge above a steep road from Llanychaer in the Gwaun val-

ley. There is nothing to see in the church, rebuilt in 1859. The architect was R. J. Withers, who, assuming that he had seen the site, should have done better justice to it. The churchyard gate-posts are faintly incised with Celtic crosses, and an overgrown holy well behind an adjacent cottage is roughly stone vaulted. Enormous boulders are embedded in the earth banks which line the lanes; opposite the entrance to

Scoveston Fort, **Llanstadwell**. One of several built (1852–70) around Milford Haven by Palmerston

the churchyard, the lane leading to the moors passes *Parc y Meirw*—the field of the dead. Here there is the biggest megalithic alignment in Wales; four enormous boulders, one broken off, still stand and four more are visible in the nearby banks. They cover in all a distance of about 50 yards and some of them are as much as 16 feet long. They are on a line with the church and it may not be too idle to suppose that they had a connection with its site. The lane from the church to the Fishguard road above Dinas is worth taking for close views of moorland and walls of loose stones, weathered and lichened to the softest of grey.

LLANRHEITHAN [5] Deep in the lanes of Dewisland. The

1862 bellcote church (architect R. K. Penson) stands almost in the farmyard of Llanrheithan farm, which has a fine slate-hung and slurried front.

LLANRIAN [4] A cross-roads cluster; cottages, school and farm with out-buildings. Rookery in the churchyard. The grey cruciform church fits well into this simple scene, with its low saddleback 13c tower at the west end, recently cleaned and repointed. The rest of the church was rebuilt in 1836 (David Evans, architect) and lightly restored in 1891. It retains most of its 1836 features, slate flags in the nave, flat roof, stained pine-panelled walls, and is well lighted through clear-glass diamond-paned windows. Ten-sided (rare) font,

decorated with shields, one bearing arms of Rhys ap Thomas, supporter of Henry Tudor. From Llanrian roads lead to Barry Island farm and so to the beach of *Traethllwyn* and to the coast villages of Porthgain and Abereiddy. The stone quarries' tall, gaunt walls and machinery at *Porthgain* are deserted, beside the narrow stone-groined harbour, and here, and around the derelict cottages of *Abereiddy*, you may feel that the atmosphere is ghostly and sinister. The plain, substantial 18c house of *Trevacoon*, grey-plastered and with more beautiful out-buildings, is on the lower road to St Davids. On the upper road at *Croes Goch* the façade of the Baptist Chapel (1816–58) once an eye-catcher in yellow and Venetian red is

Strumble Head, **Llanwnda**

now a more sober white and grey, but the pointed windows with interlaced bars and the rose window in the gable compel attention. The *Atramont Hotel* on the corner here takes its name from Ireland.

LLANSTADWELL [3] Those who live in the cottages and villas have a front-seat view of the bustle in Pembroke Dock across the water and of the shipping. Where the village tapers into Neyland the salt water almost laps the walls of the church. Extensively restored in 1876, oak fittings have been installed as memorials. The only stained glass is in east window (Kempe style); the rest is clear,

in diamond panes. Through the long lancet window of the south transept you get a good view of the estuary. There is an oil refinery at *Waterston*.

LLANSTINAN [3] The church is tucked round the side of a quarry bank as you come into Scleddau, on the A40 from Haverfordwest. The white interior shows to advantage the sharply pointed arch of the chancel, the simple vaulting and the low oblique passage from the south recess to the chancel. Churchyard circular.

LLANTOOD [3] Featureless country on Cardigan border. Church rebuilt 1820, and again

1884 (architect D. Davies). Usual simple bellcote job. It contains early-18c table in vestry and fine 14c floriated cross slab.

LLANWNDA [2] On the way here from Fishguard, aerial view of the harbour, the bays beyond and toad-shaped Dinas Head. The indifferent layout and design of a housing estate above Goodwick, known locally as "*Stop and Call*", is a poor introduction to the *Pencaer* promontory, where the coastal scenery is fierce and romantic. Relics of pre-history pervade feeling and vision. On the north side the bare and boulder-strewn land slopes gently to the

sea, and where it turns westward the white walls of *Strumble Head lighthouse* break the horizon. To the west cliffs rise to four hundred feet, and at their foot grey seals breed. The best bay is *Pwllderi*, where a tablet has been placed to the memory of *Dewi Emrys*, whose poem, "Pwllderi", in the Pembrokeshire Welsh dialect, has put into words the beauty of the scene. A private house designed to overlook the bay is now a

◁ View southwards from Garn Fawr, **Llanwnda** and (*below*) Garn Fechan, from Garn Fawr. Wall of the Iron Age fort in the foreground

County Council Youth Hostel. *Castell Mawr*, from which this house takes its name, is a bastion-shaped promontory fort commanding the approaches from the sea, and Pencaer people still talk of Danish treasure lying in the caves below. One of the best stretches of the coastal footpath is from Pwllderi towards the cliffs of Treseissyllt Farm. In places it seems barely wide enough for passage between the sheer cliff face and the cornfields behind the earthbank on which tiny flowers glitter like stars; in other places it is wide enough to contain outcrops and pockets of

rock arranged naturally to form perfect rock gardens. Lichened and weatherworn, the stone surfaces repeat in almost microscopic form the haphazard pattern of fields, earth banks and man made trails seen as you turn your gaze inland. Less than half a mile to the east, steep *Garn Fawr* rises to nearly 700 feet and is crowned by a striking stone hill-fort. It is best approached from the eastern or landward side, where three lines of ramparts connected the natural out-crops of rock. So much of the stone has been removed over the years for building cattle shelters, and the site

is now so overgrown, that the original layout of the fort is lost. The view from the top is immense, including on a clear day the Wicklow Mountains in Ireland, and Snowdon and the Lleyn peninsula in North Wales. It is said that when shadows darken the south-west slopes of Garn Fawr, the outlines of stone hut circles are visible and in the yard of the small farm of *Tol Gaer* (opposite the youth hostel) you can see the corbelled crown of a stone hut, locally described as a prehistoric sty. *Trefasser* hamlet is reputed to be the birthplace of Asser, friend and counsellor of King Alfred. Farmhouse groups in the district are solidly built against the gales and have grey slurry roofs. *Treathro*, north of Pwllderi, is a good example.

In the parish are the remains of six dolmens, and the village consists of a few houses bordering a small piece of common land strewn with larger stones, some of which were probably part of a stone circle. The church on the north-east side was carefully restored, with proper simplicity, in 1870. Medieval wooden beams over the nave, on one of which is a rude boss of a human head; lancet windows in the chancel, and plain vaulting. The interior is clear, with cream and white paint. Squint from porch to chancel.

Worshippers in the church get a view of the sea below, whence, on a fine February day in 1797, a French force, calling itself the Black Legion and recruited from prisons, landed under the command of an Irish American named Tate. His orders were to land either in the Bristol Channel or in Cardigan Bay, and strike inland. Obliged to choose the latter, he landed his troops and established his headquarters in Trehowell farm. The French raiding parties ransacked neighbouring farms and cottages, which happened to be well stocked with liquor from a recent wreck. The main force was therefore in no condition to offer much resistance to a force of Pembrokeshire militiamen, which Lord Cawdor smartly moved up from Haverfordwest, and the ensuing engagement, although it did nothing to alter the course of our island story, has given the Pembrokeshire Yeomanry the battle honour Fishguard which it proudly carries on its cap badge. The story of the Welsh women in red flannel cloaks deceiving the French by marching around a rock is probably apocryphal.

LLANYCEFN [6] Steep hillside village. Bellcote church, restored 1904. Small squint and door to rood loft.

LLANYCHAER. LLANYCHLLWYDOG. *See* GWAUN VALLEY.

LLAWHADEN [6] The early 14c castle, which became a residence of the Bishops of St Davids, is sited high. It was probably dismantled by Bishop Barlow (1536–48), and used as a quarry for building-stones until the Welsh Church Commission handed it on to what is now the Department of the Environment. A moat 70 feet wide and 25 feet deep surrounds it, and is associated with the original ring motte castle which preceded the present building. The church, old stone bridge and 18c mill, now converted to a private house, sit together by the river below. The church has two towers, the northern one the older. The other was added in the 14c to fill the gap made when part of the original nave was removed, to allow a new nave and chancel to be built on the north side. A plan in the vestry illustrates this. Norman corbels and a two-headed beast. Pattern glass, not bad, in east window. *Llawhaden House*, in centre of village, has a 17c staircase and a panelled room. Part of it is Tudor, and there is earlier stone vaulting. The farm buildings with dovecote are of good plain stone work. On high ground overlooking Canaston Bridge, *Ridgeway* stands up well. A large house of two storeys, with jutting wings under hipped roofs, and a long recessed centre, it was largely rebuilt towards the middle of the 18c and it was described by Richard Fenton who visited it about 1800. It belonged to the *Foley* family since the 14c. Five royalist Foleys were killed on nearby Colby Moor in the Civil War. Sir Thomas Foley, who led the fleet at the Battle of the Nile, came here from Abermarlais in Carmarthenshire, and he entertained Lord Nelson with Sir William and Lady Hamilton here in 1802. The last of the Foleys died in 1965. The long groundfloor room in the recessed centre is panelled. From the hall a double staircase with a single return flight of stairs leads to a passage of elegant arches on the upper floor. There are tales of phantom Foley Cavaliers galloping along the old drive.

132

LLYS Y FRAN [5] The tiny hillside church with its medieval font (claws in the angles of the base stone), but otherwise rebuilt and refitted, is still on the hillside. Below it the Pembrokeshire Water Board has dammed the *Syfynwy Valley* to form a regulating reservoir which holds 2,000 million gallons and, if needed, can be raised by 40 feet to hold 5,000 million gallons. It will control the flow of the Eastern Cleddau which is joined by the Syfynwy just below the reservoir. The best way to get to it is through Clarbeston. It enhances and gives interest to this otherwise rather featureless countryside, especially when the sheet of water is seen from a distance from, say, the Preseli hills.

LOVESTON [9] On a hilltop among grey stuccoed houses, the tall-towered church will delight anti-Victorians; medieval squints and masonry, Perpendicular windows and tiny pointed transepts go well with stone flags. Early 18c painted memorial (indecipherable) in chancel, and flattened Communion rails, within pale-green walls. Boxed in pews throughout and west end benches. Pulpit is recent, and late 18c memorial to Henry Leach is worth reading.

LUDCHURCH [6] Strange and striking site. Quarry work into the limestone on the south side of the churchyard has dramatised the levels. A curious landscape of cliffs, declivities and pools with tangled trees matted with ferns and lichen to the west, Japanese in detail. (Old quarries.) The church sits well

above all this on its green knoll. It is more interesting than most hereabouts. Outside, very characteristic of Pembrokeshire: with its battered tower and dark grey, defensive appearance. Early medieval arcade, with shields on capitals. Stoups, one with a head between two roses. Modern stained glass. Picturesque farm nearby.

LYDSTEP HAVEN [9] Fine view of Caldy Island from the shore of this well-wooded bay, now largely a caravan site. Large Victorian house in trees. Fine caves.

MAENCLOCHOG [6] This raw moorland village of stone-built cottages and corrugated iron on the edge of the Preseli hills is the centre of country well worth exploring for its steep valleys, clear, fast-running streams and wooded slopes. The church, in a raised churchyard, is mid-Victorian and dull, except for an unusual small tower at the west end capped by a gilded weathercock elegantly borne on wrought iron. Opposite, Congregational *Hên* (*old*) *Gapêl* (1790, 1870, 1904) is the most striking building in the village, with its turreted cement-rendered façade, cinema Gothick. George Owen in his *Description of Pembrokeshire* records a plague here in 1601, of "Caterpillers or greene wormes haveinge manye legges and bare without haere", which covered 200 acres. They were there for three weeks and after they had consumed all the mountain grass were themselves consumed by sea mews and crows "alfoe fwine fedd upon those wormes egerlye and waxed very

fatte", (for Rosebush *see* Preseli).

MANORBIER [9] The romantic Norman castle stands on the north slope of the valley like a Crusader castle, about half a mile from the shore, with the church set apart on the opposite slope. The castle is private, and incorporates a 19c residence within the courtyard, but it is open to the public from April to October. It is well preserved, especially the 12c gateway tower, the massive round tower in the eastern corner and the external walls. Within, the domestic buildings have gone, except for the Great Hall and the vaulted chapel. Giraldus Cambrensis (Gerald the Welshman) was born here in 1146, Norman on his father's side but Welsh through his mother, Angharad, daughter of Nesta, the Welsh Helen of Troy. As a young man he studied at Paris University and became Archdeacon of Brecon. In 1188 he toured Wales with Archbishop Baldwin seeking recruits for the Third Crusade, and recounted his experiences in his books. Gerald, largely because he was thwarted by Canterbury in his ambitions to become Bishop of St Davids, made repeated visits to Rome to have St Davids made independent of Canterbury but the Pope, although diverted by Gerald's stories and mimicry of the Archbishop's Latin howlers, was not moved by his arguments. Gerald loved Manorbier, which he wrote of as the "Paradise of all Wales".

The church in its oldest part the nave (*c.* 1150), pre-dates most of the present castle. The chancel was rebuilt, and transepts and north aisle built,

about a hundred years later. In the 14c the south aisle was added, and the north transept extended to contain the de Barri tomb, now in the chancel. The result is a clumsy medley of arches and pillars, which was not improved in the 1867 restoration by heavy and still clumsier plastering; so that the impression on entering the church down the steps from the porch is one of coming into a cavern. The 14c oak loft leading into the tower is one of the few remaining examples of medieval church woodwork in the county. There is a modern (Whitefriars) stained-glass window in the west wall. The vaulted roof of the porch has original painted patterns. Royal arms.

MANORDEIFI [3] The old church, on the left bank of the Teifi is a nave-and-chancel building, with Early English traces. Box pews, two with fireplaces, and original benches. All windows have 18c clear glass. Altar rails enclose the altar table on three sides. The passage between the pews is stone flagged, but the floorboards inside the pews have perished showing the shingle below. 13c font. Tablets, one to the memory of a soldier mauled to death by a tiger in Rawalpindi. In recent years the fabric has been made sound, the bellcote rebuilt and the fine wrought-iron enclosures to the graves are being cleaned of rust and repainted. *Benedicite Omnia Opera*. The coracle in the porch is not waiting for Charon; it was once used for rescuing prayer books and surplices from floods. The drive from this church

along the river to Abercych is varied and agreeable. The modern church, built on higher ground in 1899 (architects Protheroe and Phillpott), is conventional: high, long and narrow. Plenty of stained glass. The font and pulpit have been moved from a private chapel of the Victorian house of Pentre. They are of marble with panels of Victorian Byzantine mosaics. *Ffynnone* is the best country house north of Little England. Designed by John Nash in 1793, the south front was enlarged early in the 19c in the Greek Doric style and although the house was remodelled by Inigo Thomas in 1904, Nash's work remains inside, and the drawing-room, the staircase, and the hall and vestibule ceilings are Nash at his most elegant. Where the massive, old bridge carries the road from Cilgerran into Cardiganshire the pretty Dutch-gabled building of slate slabs is the lodge to *Castell Malgwyn*, a site of importance in ancient days, and now occupied by a late-18c plain three-storeyed block, now a hotel. Outbuildings in quadrangle with cupola. The whole built for London banker, Sir Benjamin Hammett. Fine trees in park. Sir Benjamin established a small tinplate works nearby; they were later demolished by his son and their exact location is unknown. However, the narrow canal which runs from the old church to the river bridge was connected with them.

MANOROWEN [2] Good, plain early-19c house on earlier foundations overlooks tiny Victorian church in pleasant sylvan setting.

p138 **Marloes** from above ▷
Gateholm Island
p139 **Marloes** sands

MARLOES [7] Church, cottages, a clock tower to Lord Kensington, council houses and greenhouses suggest a village on English pattern, yet the whole gives the distinctive Welsh feeling of aloofness in this corner of Little England. Marloes sands, about 15 minutes' walk from the car park, provide good bathing. Besides leaving sharp-toothed boulders in the sand, the sea has cut the cliff faces into arches and chimneys, especially where it has eaten away the upright layers of shale from the sandstone. The grey weathered church restored in 1874, on a knoll, is sombre inside and has a sunken baptistry next to the font. S.W. London names originated here, e.g. Marloes Road, Philbeach Gardens. *Philbeach Farm* has a "Flemish" chimney.

MARTLETWY [5] A few detached houses and low cottages in a tranquil, wooded hillside setting. Off centre, tall, grey Baptist chapel without inscriptions and, below, double-aisled bellcote church restored 1874 (architect E. V. Collier) has mottled grey limestone arcade, black pointed, and interesting medieval carved head of tonsured priest, facing the altar from the chancel arch; also square medieval font basin and base. Palest blue walls, and darker blue underneaths to arches. East of village, tiny *Horeb* Congregational chapel in sober grey roughcast. *Landshipping* has a romantic view across the estuary to Picton Castle (*see*

Nevern

absence of windows in the north wall and heavy stained glass in the south, but the chancel is flooded with light on to the gilded and painted reredos. The rural parish takes in much of the *Canaston* woodland, and, southwards, *Templeton*, once a stronghold of the Knights Templar and now a ribbon development hillside village, with a modest late 19c church.

NEVERN [3] The largest parish in the county, stretching from the coast north of Newport into the Preseli hills and the sheep country beyond Brynberian. The northern part is wide open pasture land, and the fine stone-built farm of *Berry Hill* indicates Norman Marcher Lordship influence (*see* Moylgrove). The village on the secondary Newport–Cardigan road is on the English pattern, church with a low tower among yew trees, school, parsonage, inn ("Trewern Arms") and narrow stone bridge over the river, all neatly grouped. There is a splendid village fete in August. Superstition says that a yew tree near the entrance gate to St Brynach's church sheds blood, and visitors flock to see the dark sap. There is more to interest them in the massive 13-feet high St Brynach's sculptured cross of the late 10 or early 11c, elaborately carved in abstract designs of plait and fret work. The stone is dolerite from nearby Preseli. Nearby stands a Latin/ Ogam inscribed stone, reputed to have come from Cwm Gloyne.

The cruciform church is late Perpendicular, the interior thoroughly restored. There is a priest's chamber over the south transept and a Latin/Ogam stone on a window sill. On the Frongoch road about 100 yards above the church, a rough cross is cut in relief on the bare rock with a natural ledge on which pilgrims to and from St Davids are supposed to have knelt. Nevern is rich in prehistoric remains, including the *Pentre Ifan dolmen* with its delicately poised capstone. At a bend of the road in the hamlet of *Velindre* is a small stone Elizabethan house, modernised but with mullioned windows. Originally a school, it is used twice a year for Courts Leet of the Barony of Cemaes. On the other side of the lane is the stone enclosed village pound. *Henllys*, the home of the Elizabethan George Owen, who wrote a description of Pembrokeshire, is now a modern building. Above Velindre to the north is a fine earthwork, *Castell Henllys*. Also to the north is the old farmhouse of *Cwm Gloyne*, originally three sides of a square: one of the wings has been demolished fairly recently. It has a Jacobean staircase, and there is reputed to be an Ogam stone behind the plaster in one of the downstairs rooms. There is a carved head on an entrance gate pillar. *Trewern*, off the road to Pentre Ifan, is another early Jacobean house with a large porch (stone seats and a slit window), oak doors, stone masonry and pine panelling. On the Cardigan road, the octagonal pink-washed building looking like a Rockingham china house is the lodge to *Llwyngwair* manor house, now a hotel. Medieval, Tudor, Georgian and good late 19c architecture and craftsmanship combine well in this pleasant house. Rhododendrons and azaleas.

St Brynach's cross,
Nevern

Newchapel (**Manordeifi**)

NEW MOAT [6] Derives its name from the motte-and-bailey Norman castle mound, now overgrown with trees, in the village centre. The countryside is wooded and uneven. The church was almost rebuilt in the 1870s, except for the south Pembrokeshire tower. To lessen draught the aisle and entrance to the tower have been boarded off. Purple and green "cathedral" glass. Font with scalloped-edged basin and tapering flutes and an early 17c altar tomb with panels and shields and tomb chest beneath, and traces of colour. The vaults, below the vestry, of the *Scourfield* family who lived at the Motte (now demolished) were recently opened. They contained 11 lead coffins from 1737 onwards in their original drapery, and the bones of a greyhound. Tradition says that the Motte was built from the proceeds of a bet on a greyhound; a greyhound figures in the Scourfield arms.

NEWPORT [3] Once an important seaport. George Owen (*see* Nevern) described it as a once populous place, and seat of the woollen industry early in the 16c, which never recovered from a visitation of the sweating sickness. Now it is regaining some prosperity as a seaside resort and the narrowness of the main coastal road through its centre creates traffic problems in the summer to which a cross-roads contributes. It is dominated by the Norman castle on a circular mound built by the Marcher Lord Martin de Tours, who established the

◁ **Newport** Baptist chapel   147

barony of Cemaes and conferred privileges on the borough which are still guarded. A modern residence was built into the ruins of the castle's 13c gatehouse in 1859. The narrow Nevern estuary divides what is left of the old port from stretches of firm yellow sands and dunes, ideal for children, and backed by a 9-hole golf course.

The port is now reduced to a tiny dock under the shadow of a rubble-built warehouse of indeterminate date (now converted into a dwelling on the ground floor) and limekilns overgrown with bushes. There is an atmosphere about this little harbour, especially out of season, and its tide-worn runnels, slime-green rocks, slatey gutters and rusty iron mooring rings and bollards. It calls to mind the village boys apprenticed to the sea and boarding the schooners for their first voyage, perhaps to settle later as master mariners on the *Parrog*, a terrace of tall sombre houses which runs at right-angles to the quay.

Tidy council house development partly separates the harbour from the rising ground, where full of character the streets and lanes below the castle walls are narrow and have some small Georgian houses and cottage rows with many bay windows. Up to the skyline the pastures and dark moorland dotted with whitewashed cottages form a theatrical background which no other place in the county can rival.

The church is massive on the original Norman pattern, cruciform, lofty and with plenty of light and space. The buttressed tower is 13c, and the rest was

completely restored in 1879 by the Cheltenham architect Middleton. Absence of plaster on the walls is compensated for by the excellent masonry in local igneous stone of shades of grey and palest brown. Windows in chancel by Heaton and Butler incorporate earlier medallions. Across from the north-east churchyard gate a tiny 1799 chapel with original furniture, now an adjunct of the parish church, marks the local origin of the Methodist movement, which split from the church when some members demanded that the Sacrament should be administered by their own ministers rather than in the parish church. The *Baptist chapel* (1789–1855) and Congregational *Ebenezer* (1845) are both buildings with a presence. To the south the heights of the steep crag of *Carn Ingli* were converted by Iron Age man into a stone-enclosed camp. The Megalithic men have left one dolmen, *Goetan Arthur* in a cottage paddock on the way down to the estuary bridge and, outside the village on the right-hand side of the Dinas road in a dip, a larger one or group, now considerably disturbed, probably by Fenton (*see* Fishguard).

NEYLAND [8] Brunel had plans for an important railway terminal here and the ships to Ireland used the port until their transfer to Fishguard in 1906. There is a terrace named after Brunel's *Great Eastern*. Neyland has declined compared with neighbouring Milford and Pembroke Dock, although a new Technical College has been opened. The parish church, built in the early 1930s (archi-

tect Ellery-Anderson), is plain and well lit.

NOLTON *Nolton Haven* is a grassy, brackeny inlet with a farm, cottages and a classic stone chapel (1858) with gallery. The village, a little inland from the coast, has farmhouses, church, old school and rookery. The bellcote church, restored in 1876, is simple. The porch has a white-ribbed vaulted roof similar to the one at neighbouring Roch, and a stone effigy of a mail-clad figure whose appearance (and dignity) has suffered from service as a gatepost. Clear windows inside and tiled floor. Curious stone bracket, probably Norman but with Celtic influence, on north wall of nave; on the face side three heads are carved, one bearded, and on the east side animal figures, perhaps a greyhound chasing a hare, and on the west side a ribbon decoration. Springtime, pink primroses in churchyard. On the road to Lambston there are eastward views with Preseli in the background.

PEMBROKE [8] The Castle is to Pembroke as the Cathedral is to St Davids. It is sited on a rugged, in places almost vertical, limestone rock at the western edge of a ridge overlooking the Pembroke river, an almost land-locked inlet of Milford Haven. It was chosen by the Normans very soon after the Conquest as their base against Ireland and the Welsh, easily defended, and reinforced by sea. By 1093 a palisaded fortress had been built and a ditch dug across the headland. Pembroke became a County Palatine in 1138 and Gilbert de Clare

(Strongbow) was the first Earl Palatine. He was followed by a succession of Norman war lords—Marshall, de Valence, Hastings and Herbert among them. The Marshall family built the castle largely as it is to-day, including the Great Keep, between 1189 and 1245; the existing fort was incorporated in the Inner Ward. On the north side there is natural access at salt-water level to the Inner Ward through *Wogan's Cave*, 70-feet long by 50-feet wide, from which steps lead up to the Northern Hall. Henry Tudor, later Henry VII, was born in the Castle in 1457. His son Henry VIII abolished the Palatinate in his Act of Union. In the later stages of the Civil War (1648) Cromwell in person laid siege to the Castle, stubbornly defended by Mayor Poyer, himself a former Parliamentarian. Hunger compelled its surrender and Poyer fell before a firing squad in Covent Garden in 1649. Private restoration was carried out in 1880, and after frequent changes of hands the Castle was leased to the Borough Council. Architecturally, the glory of the Castle is the *Great Keep*, built by Strongbow or by William Marshall. It is over 100-feet high, built of rough limestone without buttress support and ending in a stone dome; the walls at the base are over 19 feet thick. It originally had a basement and four storeys. It is unique among Norman keeps in Britain or France. As a town developed outside the Castle walls and along the landward route to it, the citizens in times of trouble retreated within them, until in the more peaceful days of the

15c a wall was thrown from the west gate of the Castle and another from the north gate to take in both sides of the main thoroughfare to a point about three miles from the Castle. The river protected them on one side and marshland on the other. Few traces remain—part of the West gate near the Castle remains on Monkton Hill where there are medieval houses. The pattern of the town to-day is still one of a long medieval thoroughfare leading to the Castle, lined now with shops, houses and hotels all rather grey in tone and almost blocked at its eastern end by the forbidding façade of a Methodist chapel. Their irregular roof-line is emphasised by a slight dip in the ground. Behind the houses and shops on the south side of this street is a steepish slope which accommodates their gardens and these are bounded at the bottom of the slope by the ruins of one of the medieval walls. If you come into the town from the south these gardens and walls are a very attractive feature. With the trees on the flat open ground at the bottom (traversed by the by-pass road), the scene has a look of a country town in central or southern France.

There are two parish churches, the best is St Mary's, built in the 13c and considerably restored since, high-aisled, with some tablets from the early 17c onwards. St Michaels was built in 1832 (T. Rowlands architect; restored by Lingen Barker 1887). The lonely tower and steepled church on *Windmill Hill*, south-west of the town, is open only on special occasions. There is a view from the

Castle of *Bush House*, now a school. All that is left of the Georgian House described by Fenton are low terrace wings. It was burnt down and rebuilt in stone with Tudor-style windows in 1906 (joint architects were Morgan of Carmarthen and Lloyd Oswell of Shrewsbury).

PEMBROKE DOCK [8] A small obelisk in *Albion Square* records that the Royal Dockyard was established in 1814. The first ships built were the *Valorous* and *Ariadne*, both launched on February 10th, 1816, and "the town was built almost entirely by the working classes who by their thrift and industry erected during the century upwards of 2000 houses". The latter were laid out on the gridiron pattern and the long regular lines of oriel windows can be monotonous. The Dockyard is now on a care and maintenance basis and there is talk of it becoming a base for drilling operations for oil and gas in the Irish Sea. St John's church was built in 1848 (architect J. P. Harrison). The *Warrior* lies at the M.O.D. (Navy) Llanion Oil Fuel Depot off the main road to the new bridge at Waterloo. Now used as an oil pontoon, she was the first iron-clad warship, laid down in 1859. 380 feet long, she displaced 10,000 tons and had sail propulsion as well as steam. Schemes have been put forward to turn her into a museum. You cannot see her without a pass from the Naval Dockyard at the other end of the town and to get to Llanion you have to pass a terrible rubbish dump. You can see the seagulls scavenging from miles away.

Pembroke

PENALLY [9] On a hillside overlooking Tenby golf course and the sea. Regency and earlier houses. St Teilo, contemporary of St David, laboured here. The church has a famous sculptured cross, now moved from the churchyard into the south transept where an all-round view is impossible. It is a monolith, dating from about the 11c and, standing six feet high, is the smallest and best proportioned of the three such crosses in the county. The wheel-head is elaborately carved with twisted cords around a central boss. The upper part of the shaft face reflects Northumbrian influence in the conventionalised single vine scroll and bunches of grapes; the lower part is covered in abstract plait and knot work. Also in the church is a fragment of a cross shaft on which, difficult to discern, are two identical animals, facing each other and of Northumbrian influence. Behind the Penally Arms hotel are the medieval ruins of St Deiniol's chapel.

PENRHUDD [3] On eastern flank of the Preseli range the tiny 1841 church in an overhung setting of yew trees was restored in 1910, but the benches remain in the chancel. It is now used only for harvest festivals and special occasions.

Plump verdigris weathercock above bellcote.

PONTFAEN. *See* GWAUN VALLEY.

PRENDERGAST [5] A parish in its own right, now a suburb of Haverfordwest. The church, rebuilt, except for Norman tower, in 1876 (architect J. Foster, brother of the then rector), is spacious and well designed. 17 and 18c monuments. Window by Powell (Whitefriars) and a good deal of other stained glass.

PRESELI [6] This range of hills falls like a shadow across most of the county from north-east to south-west, for the most part a bleak moorland of sparse heather, gorse, and boulders with a few rocky crags, on which 60 inches of rain a year fall. Bogs indicate underlying deposits of boulder clay but for the most part the rocks are slates and grits with interbedded igneous rocks such as dolerite and rhyolite, the "blue" stones of Stonehenge. Summer grazing for sheep which are wintered on the firing-range of Castlemartin, and, all the year, mountain ponies. Grazing rights are as jealously guarded by courts leet as verderers' rights in the New Forest. Much of the lower slopes has been enclosed and brought under

cultivation, and there are large forestry plantations on the south slopes. At the sad village of *Rosebush* (disused quarries), is the abandoned Clynderwen Maenclochog railway opened in 1876; also a reservoir with trout fishing. The quarries closed before 1914. There are immense views from the higher points; the highest, at 1760 feet, is *Foel Cwmcerwyn*. The road from Eglwyswrw in the north to Haverfordwest gives a good idea of the landscape, which everywhere is dotted with cairns of prehistoric man. Ingenious suggestions are put forward from time to time as to how the megalithic builders moved the Stonehenge blue

stones to Salisbury Plain, but much new evidence about glaciation in south-west England during the Ice Ages suggests that the stones could have been carried from South Wales or even further by the ice.

The leaflet *The Preseli Hills* by John Barrett and Neville Penry Thomas published by the National Parks Committee (*see* Introduction) is an admirable guide to all aspects of the area. (*See* also Meline and Whitechurch.)

PUNCHESTON [5] Good centre for the moorland country, otherwise a rather dreary village in which a row of houses called Park Avenue may raise a smile. Church rebuilt in 1895 by E. V. Collier. The nearby hamlet of *Castleblythe* is worth a diversion for tree shade and the

Norman motte castle. Modern farm buildings and English are encroaching on a place that was so firmly Welsh a few years ago that English was hardly understood. A church almost completely rebuilt in 1875 is no longer in use, and in fact almost impossible to get to.

PWLLCROCHAN [8] A Celtic name, like its neighbour's, Rhoscrowther. A weathered, cruciform, 14c church with small tower and spire, mid-19c furnishings: semi box pews with doors, clear glass throughout and slate floors. A well of very pure water in the churchyard, among trees running down to the cocklebeds of Milford Haven. Sounds idyllic, but the farm ground above is now occupied by the columns, towers, and tanks of a nearby refinery

◁ **Pembroke Dock**

below Warrior, the first ironclad warship, **Pembroke Dock**

and the cockles stir uneasily in their mud. The Pembroke Electricity Power Station is a recent neighbour, on partly reclaimed ground at *West Pennar*. Its chimney stacks—the tallest is 714 feet—add a new dimension to the landscape. It has four 500 MW turbo generators each of which can generate more electricity than Battersea Power Station. It is the largest oil-fired power station in Europe.

REDBERTH [9] Closely grouped houses and cottages, many pink-washed, on A477. Tall houses with pointed chapel-type windows overlooks toy-fort tower of 1844 church by George Brown. F. R. Kempson in 1913 alterations mercifully preserved the low-doored pews, miniature, almost two-decker, pulpit and adjacent reading desk, three-sided Communion rails, Commandment tablets on either side of altar, benches in chancel and clear-glass, lattice windows. All woodwork is in contrasting shades of brown. A good period piece.

REYNALTON [9] A single-chamber, stone-flagged, and towered church looking across the valley and up at Loveston. Interior primitive, but without character. Village shows traces of abandoned anthracite mining.

RHOSCROWTHER [8] Tanks of oil refinery installations; otherwise open country, almost on the shore of Angle Bay. A valley settlement of church, rectory (now a guest house), cottages, and council houses on the hillside. The church is dedicated to St Decuman, reputed to have

been born here and to have crossed the Severn in a coracle landing near Dunster in Somerset where he lived as a hermit until his martyrdom in 706.

W. D. Caröe renovated the church about 1910 after a 19c restoration in which all windows were replaced in incongruous Bath stone. Irregular in plan and alignment, typical of south Pembrokeshire churches, it consists of nave and chancel, probably 13c, 14c transepts (the south one is the ground storey of the tower) and a chapel south of the chancel. Under a separate roof, an annexe on the south-west side once connected to a south porch which was removed at some uncertain date and rebuilt with stone seats and cobbled floor as a large north porch on a line with the north transept. Caröe suggested in his notes that this annexe is an earlier building, possibly the site of St Decuman's cell. The inside walls and the diagonal passages which connect transepts with the chancel and side chapel are white-washed and heavily plastered. Blue and cream tiled flooring. The font of Caen stone is Norman. A recess in the north wall of the chancel a 14c richly decorated monument. A grotesque medieval figure about 12 inches high has been mounted over the pointed arch of the north porch. Its history is unknown and its upraised hands and crowned head suggest the risen Christ. *Eastington* on the edge of another oil refinery is a long-fronted farmhouse with a square tower and parapet (probably 15c) on its seaward side.

ROBESTON WATHEN [6] A cluster of houses below the tall 13c tower of a church decently Victorianised. *Canaston Bridge* where the main road branches to Tenby and Pembroke is early 17c.

ROBESTON WEST [8] The southern part will be taken up by the tank farm of a proposed oil refinery almost up to the church (near a pond and a ferny well). To the original early Norman building a southern aisle, now the nave and chancel, was added, probably in the 14c. The original part, now the north aisle, and the tower, are very much in their primitive state and have stone-flagged floors bare of seating, and stone altar. New roof. The pointed arches dividing the two chambers are coloured blue-grey. Walls are cream and white, and clear-glass windows give plenty of light. Early effigy, and Roch family tablets. An attractive church. Primroses in the spring, including the pink varieties, so common in the county. Walls, arches, gateposts and tumbled spaces of a vanished house nearby.

ROCH [5] The 13c peel tower rises from an out-crop of rock like a fairy tale illustration. It can be seen for miles and is in the centre of an attractive village. It was cleverly converted into a private house at the beginning of this century. The church was rebuilt except for the porch, which has a stone-ribbed vaulted roof, about 1860 (architect R. K. Penson). Raised, circular churchyard. Nave and chancel are darkened by heavy stained glass, mainly

Trefran colliery **(Roch)**

early 20c, in all windows except one. Two and a half miles east of Roch, Newgale Sands stretch four miles, cut off at the northern end from the road by a high shingle bank. Remains (chimney and engine house) of colliery workings at Trefran.

◁ Newgale Sands
(Roch)

ROSEBUSH. *See* PRESELI.

ROSEMARKET [8] The home of Lucy Walter, mother of the Duke of Monmouth. Small village with Celtic-type church of 1891 in very ordinary countryside.

RUDBAXTON [5] Castle mound and banks with farm inside them. The outside of the lonely

church has weathered into an agreeable grey tone suited to the charming landscape, and the squat tower is a pleasant change from the tall fortified towers to the south. One of the least spoiled late-Victorian interiors in the county. The furnishings are all of a piece, except for the very quaint rustic Baroque monument (late 17c) to the Howard family, with four

157

Crundale rath, **Rudbaxton**

almost life-sized figures. Also Picton monuments. A south aisle was added in the 14c and two plain obtuse arches on a central circular column divide it from the nave. The east window is modern and except for a single lancet in the chancel all other windows are square-headed Perpendicular. 20c brass to Archbishop Laud, who was pluralist rector 1622–1626. 13c font. *Poyston Hall*, a small three-storeyed Georgian block in the trees at the back of Withybush Aerodrome was the

early home of General Sir Thomas Picton, killed at Waterloo in command of the British 5th Division.

ST BRIDES [4] A small beach in red sandstone, with a church, a limekiln (ships used to put in here) and two houses, one the rectory. Running inland is a long stone wall, broken by cottages and corbelled out in places, which formerly enclosed a monastic garden, now a huge rookery. The church was thoroughly restored in the

1860s by E. H. Lingen Barker, but the steps and ogee-arched doorway from the chancel to the rood-loft were left. All the windows are heavily stained, and in spite of white-plastered walls the interior is dark. Tenby museum has flint implements found on Nab Head. The late Victorian baronial residence on the hillside, once the seat of the Kensington family, conceals traces of an earlier house and is now a county hospital. It looks fine from the beach, but not so good close to.

Howard monument, **Rudbaxton** ▷

ST DAVIDS [4] David, Dewi, patron saint of Wales, founded a monastery here about 520. The promontory is known as Dewisland. The landscape is bare and windswept, with outcrops of rock, and clumps of trees struggling to shelter isolated farms. The site of the Cathedral of St David is both unusual and exciting—a fold of the ground in this desolate landscape, which obscures it from distant views. The pinnacles on the top stage of the tower (added in the 16c when danger from raiders was over) are all that can be seen even across the open country to the north-west.

To the medieval Englishman this was the end of the world. Two pilgrimages to St Davids equalled one to Rome. It was a great effort indeed to get here at all. The cathedral 'city', or village, lies above the site of the monastic community. It has a main street, two cross streets, and some modern development outwards, especially towards the west, and the whole has a white, beige and grey personality, without distinction in its individual houses.

Standing in the Tower Gate—the main entrance to the Cathedral Close, and part of an immense fortified wall—you look down on the roofs of the Cathedral and on to the quadrangle of the Bishop's Palace. Palace and wall were built by Bishop Gower in the 14c. The impressive arcaded parapet of the Palace, of many open arches of alternate purple and yellow stone, and the archway and rose

Porth Clais, **St Davids**

window of the Great Hall make a rich display, and catch all eyes beside the plain exterior of the Cathedral, especially the cold west front that faces them. John Nash rebuilt this front in 1789 when it was about to collapse from the outward pressure of the Norman arches. Sir Gilbert Scott rebuilt it again in 1863, from drawings of the original.

But if the exterior is plain the interior is rich in colour, mood and detail. The first impression is of the velvety lilac-coloured bloom of the elaborate late-Norman arcades, six bays orna-mented with chevron and other ornament, clerestory and tri-forium; and of the 16c Irish oak ceiling of the nave, with pendants—"of almost Arabian gorgeousness", as *Murray's Handbook* remarks. There is a general effect of stonework and woodwork combining in a light and handsome setting. There is a violent slope upwards from west to east—the High Altar is fourteen feet higher than the west door—which gives a strange rustic personality to this highly wrought interior. You feel that the strong and wild outside landscape has possessed the building, and that you are here more as a pilgrim than a sightseer, so strong and indivi-dual is the atmosphere. An enclosed passage leads through the double walls of the 14c stone screen to the choir, with its fine, late-15c choir stalls. The tran-septs were rebuilt after the fall of the tower in 1220. Twenty-eight years later, an earthquake caused further damage. Three Early English windows over the High Altar are elaborately carved, and have Salviati mosaics inserted in them. They were repaired with lighter-coloured stone after the earthquake shock. The most delicate feature of the building is the 16c fan-vaulted ceiling in Cotswold stone of the Holy Trinity chapel. There is glass of the 19 and 20c—the best of it earlyish, and by Hardman. Butterfield as well as Scott was a restorer. On the north side of the Cathedral, St Mary's College, a 13c building, which had long been derelict, was restored under the direction of the Cathedral Architect, A. Caröe, and opened in 1966 as the Cathedral equivalent of a church hall. It is reassuring to know that tests have shown that up to July 1972 there was no clear evidence of damage being done to the Cathedral by 15 of the 16 supersonic flights of Concorde over it, and that the effect of sonic booms on foundation walls and windows and towers was often less than that of gales, although on high pitched roofs (the Cathedral nave roof is not one) the effect could be three times greater.

There is only one beach near the town that is accessible by road—*Whitesands Bay*, with a mile of sand. Less accessible coves lie below multi-coloured cliffs noticeable at *Caerfai*, from which the Normans quarried the purple sandstone of the Cathedral. West of Caerfai and due south of the town the slight remains of *St Nons chapel* stand almost on the shore of St Nons Bay with a vaulted well a few yards away. St Non was the mother of St David and the site of her chapel is reputed to have been his birthplace. The station

Standing stone, St Non's Bay
St Non's Well **(St Davids)**

St Edrens

of the famous St Davids lifeboat is at *Porthstinan*, near the ruined chapel of St Justinian, friend of St David. Opposite Porthstinan, with a narrow and dangerous race of water between, is *Ramsey Island*—farm land privately owned. Seaward from Ramsey is the line of the perilous *Bishops and Clerks rocks*.

ST DOGMAELS [3] Fishing village, where the tradition of blessing the nets has been revived. Enlarged over the last 150 years by terraces and villas

built for sea captains' retirement. Ruined abbey, founded early in the 12c and now being saved from continuing disrepair by the Department of the Environment. Recessed in a wall of the north transept is a skeleton effigy. Part of the abbey site is occupied by the parish churchyard, in which silver emblems and lettering on black tombstones contrast strangely with Norman masonry. The church (1850) is spacious and lofty. Light from tinted glass windows, a minimum of stained

glass, cream and white walls, pine pews. Cast-iron poppy heads fitted into choir stalls.

The road to the coastguard station at Cemaes Head passes through a caravan camp at *Poppit Sands*. The camp has a shop and large restaurant.

ST DOGWELLS [5] Wooded valley. View of the 18c front of *Sealyham Hall*, once the seat of the Edwardes family who first bred the Sealyham terrier. The churchyard sleeps to the sound of running water among the rhododendrons and Irish yews. The nave and chancel of the church are 13c and the south aisle is about a hundred years later. The connecting arches, two in the nave and two in the chancel, are similar to those at Rudbaxton, but the pier capitals are more elaborate.

ST EDRENS [5] A sad, towered church of 1846 with carved and incised crosses inside. Circular churchyard, the grass of which, locals say, is efficacious against rabies. Very much off the beaten track.

ST FLORENCE [9] A compact village grouped around the church. Some of the houses are old and some are gaily colour-washed council houses. One of the older houses has a "Flemish" chimney on the roadside. The cruciform Norman church has a plain tall tower. Restored in the 1870s. Chancel and south transept arches are impressively high and pointed; those from south chapel to chancel low and rounded; all are primitive. Diagonal passage from south transept, plain vaulting. 17 and 18c monuments against white walls. Benefaction board in porch.

ST ISHMAELS [7] A straggling village, still expanding. Church is away from it all in a small, remote, seaward valley among rock and ivy, blown trees, flowering shrubs and bamboos. Part of the churchyard is on the hillside, and a willow-pattern footbridge crosses the stream that separates it from the rest. This setting and the weathered red and purple stone walls of this simple building make it most attractive outside. Inside,

St Edrens

it is dark and cool because the trees exclude the light and the walls are biscuit-coloured and the pews dark. But it has atmosphere; quite a Victorian beau-ideal. The windows have clear glass in diamond panes with red and blue borders. Usual diagonal passages from transepts to chancel. Norman font. Enormous anchor, more than 17 feet long, on the lawn of Great Hoaten farmhouse (on the road to Talbenny and Little Haven). It was found on St Bride's beach and is not, as popularly sup-

posed, an Armada relic. It is of a type used in the 18c by fighting ships and large merchant-men.

ST ISSELLS. *See* SAUNDERS-FOOT.

ST LAWRENCE [5] There is a pleasant valley settlement of old and new houses at *Welsh Hook* with a mink farm (formerly trout hatchery) by the long stone bridge. Up the hill to the west above the wooded valley is the nave-and-chancel church,

165

restored in 1877, as simple inside as outside; clear-glass windows, cream walls, slate flags in the nave.

ST NICHOLAS [2] This parish on the edge of Pencaer peninsula is a mixture of moorland and well-farmed fields. Fine dolmen of *Trellys*. (The capstone has been replaced.) The church is in the centre of the village and was restored without ostentation in 1865. Tiny vaulted south transept, and curiously-arched passage from it to the chancel. Pleasantly plain and light inside. In season the churchyard is scented by winter heliotrope.

ST PETROX [8] Modern redsandstone, nave and chancel with a sanctus bellcote, tacked on to a finely weathered limestone tower. On a hilltop. Cream and slate-grey inside, and there is an elaborate coat of arms over the 1692 memorial to the Mansell family. Hereabouts notices in German, Verboten dis und Verboten dat, betoken presence of German Panzer troops, training in nearby Castlemartin.

ST TWYNELL'S [8] Gale-driven place overlooking the tank and artillery ranges of Castlemartin. Lichen-whitened tower on a Victorianised little church.

SAUNDERSFOOT [9] Is in the parish of *St Issell* and best approached from the north by a branch off the main road to Tenby near Saundersfoot station. This takes you through the beautiful wooded hollow in which St Issell's church stands. Extensive restoration by F. R.

Kempson in 1864 has given the interior the usual Victorian flavour. Typical Pembrokeshire tower, probably 14c. Early English arches in nave and chancel. Norman font of Caen type stone with carved upturned face on angle of square granite base. The site is romantic rising steeply to the east, undulating and beautified by trees. Summer visitors swell the congregation. Saundersfoot has a harbour sheltered by wooded slopes and much used by summer yachtsmen; also a large car park, amenities, garish amusement arcade and dominant, battlemented inn. It once had a trade in the export of anthracite. The deposits were largely worked by the Vickerman family, who rebuilt Hean Castle, now the home of Lord Merthyr, in 1876.

SKOKHOLM, GRASSHOLM and SKOMER ISLANDS [7] *Grassholm* (21 acres) is the smallest and the farthest, 10 miles, offshore. It is renowned for its huge colony of gannets. *Skokholm* (242 acres of red sandstone) has one of Britain's most famous bird observatories. Thousands of migratory birds are ringed on the island each year. It is the breeding ground of great numbers of Manx Shearwaters. Enquiries for visiting the Observatory should be addressed to Mr Dillwyn Miles, West Wales Naturalist Trust. (*See* Introduction.) *Skomer* (722 acres of igneous rocks) is the largest and most accessible—by boat daily between mid-March and mid-October from Martins Haven, Marloes. There is a landing charge. Dogs are not allowed. Certain parts of the island are

closed to the public. Skomer is famous for its puffins, and it has a species of vole, *Clethrionomys glareolus skomerensis*, unique to the island. Grey seals can be seen. As well as gannets, shearwaters and puffins, on the cliffs of Skokholm and Skomer guillemots and razor bills are breeding. Stormpetrels nest among loose stones and in the field walls. Herring gulls occupy niches on the cliffs; great blackbacked gulls are on the rock outcrops, and the lesser blackbacked amongst the bluebells away from the cliffs. Kittiwakes, fulmars and choughs all breed on Skomer. Cormorants, shags, oyster catchers, curlew, wheatears, raven, jackdaws, pipits and larks are regular inhabitants. Across these islands in spring and again in autumn floods the stream of migrant birds moving along the Atlantic coast of Britain.

In their own way the flowers outshine the beauty and wonder of the birds—fields of bluebells, drifts on the cliffs of ox-eye daisy, sea campion or scurvy grass. The colours of the massed tussocks of thrift along the windward cliffs shade from palest pink to deepest crimson, and only just below are vivid encrusting splashes of orange lichens. Later in the year thyme, bird's-foot trefoil, cinquefoil, speedwell, lady's bedstraw, knapweed and cat's-ear sprinkle purples and yellows amongst the grasses.

SKOMER. *See* SKOKHOLM.

SLEBECH [5] The Picton and Slebech estates overlook the Eastern Cleddau and take up most of the parish. *Picton Castle*

has remained in the possession of his direct descendants since it was built about 1300 by Sir John Wogan, who came of a Welsh family, took a Norman wife, and acquired a fortune as Justiciary (Governor) of Ireland from 1295 to 1313. Apart from the addition of a west wing, it has seen little subsequent alteration externally. The curtain walls with projecting circular towers to give crossfire against attack represent a partial advance in Norman military architecture from the massive square or circular keep. In 1750 the interior was extensively remodelled in the current classical vogue, with sash windows replacing the remaining medieval ones, new plasterwork, panelling, and fireplaces. All correspondence on these changes has disappeared, but the owner, Sir John Phillips, kept a list of letters which records one (1752) from a James Gibbs, London. It is conjectural whether the writer was the architect of that name and, if so, whether he was associated with the work. The list also records letters to and from the sculptor Henry Cheere (later Sir Henry) with a reference to fireplaces. Four marble mantelpieces at Picton can almost certainly be attributed to him. Their entablatures are carved in relief with animals, cherubs and hunting scenes. The private chapel was also remodelled, with box pews, communion rails and an organ dated 1750 by Snezler, the walls and arches to be mildly Victorianized later with painted texts and scrolls. The west wing was added about 1800 by the first Lord Milford. It is a plain castellated block of four storeys with corner turrets. The architect is not known but the rooms are exceptionally elegant and reflect the later Greek revival from George Dance junior through Soane to John Nash. Nor is an architect recorded for the Norman Revival doorway to the Castle, added between 1830 and 1840 or the stable block in the same style. The grounds and castle are open to the public on special occasions only, usually in May or June.

In neighbouring *Slebech Park* are the ruins of the church of the medieval Commandery of the Knights of St John of Jerusalem. The main walls, arches, and tower are fairly intact. There are early English and later details and patching in 18c brick. Through the open arch of the east window there is a view down the broad expanse of the tital Eastern Cleddau and the woods on the opposite bank. A service is held in the ruins on St John the Baptist's day, the last Sunday in June. At low tide appear the remains of the causeway to the Hospitallers' farm on the other side of the river. *Slebech Hall* is on the site of the Commandery. It is an impressive building of the 1770s, decastellated and with deep rounded bays at each corner, a domesticated fairy castle. It came by marriage in 1830 to the de Rutzen family from the Baltic province of Russian Courland. The de Rutzens contributed largely to the building of the present parish church, completed in 1844 (architect J. H. Good, Hatton Gardens, London). It rises in strange Gothic aloofness beside A40 and its upkeep must impose a severe strain on its members. To save cost the plaster has been scraped from the porous walls. Royal arms over the chancel arch and de Rutzen arms over the entrance.

SOLVA [4] Designed by Nature to be an artists' colony. Tiny sheltered harbour with just enough clearance between headlands to keep it open to the sea. A hundred years ago emigrants sailed from here to New York (fare £3 single, and they took their food with them). Now popular as a holiday resort and a place for lobsters and retired sea salts. Road through Solva valley runs past pink-washed cottages to Middle Mill (*see* Whitchurch). The 1877 church on the hill to the north of Solva was designed by J. L. Pearson. It follows the conventional bellcote, single aisle pattern. The absence of a chancel arch gives the interior a distinctive style and so, with less fortunate results, does the contrast, inside and out, of raw red brick with local stone.

SPITTAL [5] Scattered village. Due north, over 40 varieties of birds, mainly waterfowl, can be seen together in the aviary at *Triffleton*.

STACKPOLE [8] The Stackpole estate came to the Campbell family of Cawdor early in the 18c, when Elizabeth, sister and heir of Sir Gilbert Lort, married Sir Alexander Campbell. Stackpole Court, built in 1735 on an earlier site on severely classical lines, was demolished about 10 years ago. There has been much tree felling and replanting. The village with its dormer windows and cottages looks very well. Noticeable absence of licensed premises in these parts. There is a road to *Stackpole Quay*, which is rocky and has a stone jetty, and from there a footpath along the cliffs takes you to *Barafundle Bay*, with a scramble down to the sand. Coast views. The church, in the hamlet of *Stackpole Elidor*, lies in a watery valley by felled woods. The banked churchyard has primroses, violets and purple orchids, and the lychgate is *art nouveau*, with lead panels and cresting (1898). The church with ivied Norman tower, nave (rebuilt 1851), and original vaulted transepts has fine monuments of Richard de Stackpole and his wife with elaborate well-preserved 14c carving. Two Cawdor family hatchments on the wall of nave. Rib-vaulted (14c) Lort chapel behind choir pews on the south side contains two early 14c female effigies, an early 17c monument with the painted, kneeling figures in relief of Roger Lort, his wife and twelve children in the lower panel, seven boys on the left facing five girls on the right; and the tomb and recumbent effigy of John Frederick Campbell, first Earl Cawdor (died 1860) by John Forsyth. Modern encaustic tiles at the east end clash with the chancel effigies. There is 19c stained glass in the east and west windows. The glass in the south windows is semi-opaque with etched leaf pattern. All very 19c and proper.

STEYNTON [8] Now almost a suburb of Milford. The tall-towered church rises above the main road. A drastic 1882 res-

toration (when a human thigh bone was found in each pillar of the arcade) has left a gaunt and rather featureless interior.

TALBENNY [4] Much of the last war debris has been cleared; what is left is useful to farmers. The plain bellcote church is remote from any village centre. Inside a light, bare chancel and nave. No stalls in the chancel, only medieval stone benches along the north and south walls.

TEMPLETON. *See* NARBERTH.

TENBY [9] Sir William Paxton (*see* Llanarthney, Carmarthenshire) took Tenby in hand in 1806 and began to convert it from a decaying medieval port into the charming seaside town it is now. It is known that he employed the architect S. P. Cockerell and that the *Public Baths*, now *Laston House*, at the lower end of St Julian's Street are his work. An inscription in Greek cut into the stone above the entrance declares that "the sea washes away all human ills". No other building can definitely be attributed to Cockerell; the series of arches now rather sadly slighted cut into the cliff face above the harbour, suggest his work. Nature helped Paxton for the harbour site is beautiful. *Castle Hill*, which has the keep of the Norman Castle turned into a museum and a statue of *Prince Albert*, gives the place its special character, for it divides its splendid sandy beach into two. *South Beach* has rocky cliffs and a view of Caldy Island and the open sea, and west of it are the dunes and golf course; *North*

Beach has the harbour and a view over the bay to the Gower Peninsula. Off the dividing point is *St Catherine's Rock* with a 19c house made out of a fort, isolated at high tide. Boats ply to Caldy in the summer and on the way you get the best view of Tenby and its esplanade. It is a walled town, the fortifications 13c, enlarged in the 15c and partly rebuilt in 1588. Five arches below the tower of the south gate carry the traffic at odd angles in and out of the shopping centre. Inside the walls the layout of narrow streets and crooked lanes is medieval except for the broader High Street. Few signs are left of medieval building; here and there a projecting upper storey on corbels and in *Bridge Street* above the harbour the *Tudor Merchant's House*, now National Trust property, is open to the public in the summer. It is an example of a late 15c merchant's house with a fine "Flemish" chimney and remains of fresco wall paintings. Tenby has been proudly preserved by its townspeople as a good example of late Georgian to early Victorian architecture. Some of the painted terrace houses are as gay as a striped awning; particularly attractive is the view from Crackwell Street of *St Julian's Street* as it curves down to near harbour level. Also *St Julians Terrace* is the best terrace of late Georgian houses in west Wales. In *Crackwell Street*, *Brother Thomas' Memorial Garden* is a tribute to the memory of the Steward of Caldy Island who died recently and who was such a well-known and loved character. The houses along High Street and the Norton above the

South Beach are run-of-the-mill seaside except for *number 3 High Street*, till recently an antique shop. Mid-Victorian, of stone with three small balconies, it has an architectural personality. It was once known as the *Prize House*; its design by a Bath architect won a prize in a competition connected with the Great Exhibition. It was assembled in Tenby from marked stones shipped from Bath. John Nash designed *Sion House* on the far side of the South Beach, but it was burnt down in the 1930s and a block of flats takes its place. The medieval tower and spire of *St Mary's church* is a landmark. Plainish outside, it has an elegant arcade of eight 14c arches along the north and north-east aisles and a 15c wagon roof above the chancel and sanctuary. The sanctuary is raised by 10 steps. There is a panel of medieval glass (west window). Medieval tombs: White family in St Anne's chapel, and later tombs of Margaret Mercer and her husband Thomas ap Rees at the east end of the north aisle. 17c medallion to Robert Recorde, who invented the algebraic symbol for equality.

Augustus John is Tenby's most famous son. The *Roman Catholic church of Holyrood and St Teilo* in St Florence Parade glows with colour inside (1886, architect, F. A. Walters). In Lower Frog Street the *Welsh Presbyterian chapel*, undated, has a neat white-washed front.

Outside Tenby, John Nash is supposed to have had a hand in designing the limekilns on the *Kiln Park caravan site* off the road to Manorbier. They are in two

Tenby

Tenby

blocks; one has five main arch-ways (pointed) and the other six (round). They are stone-built, in good condition and quite impressive.

TREFFGARNE [5] The Hall built in 1824 stands well on the hill-side west of A40, and south of the gorge where the road, rail-way and river are squeezed

together between the iron-red rocks and heather. Above, wind and rain and frost have eroded the out-crops into nightmare shapes, which look from the east, in some lights, like a fan-tastic giant sculpturing a lion and unicorn.

TREVINE [4] A large (for Wales), compact, and cruci-

form village built on a rock. It lies about a mile from the sea. There is a good salty pub in this nest of deep-sea sailors.

UPTON [8] The remains of a small Norman castle have been converted into a private house which is not open to the public. It has gardens, and what was a private chapel contains sepulchral monuments of the Malefant family, and a Jacobean pulpit from St Mary's, Haverfordwest.

UZMASTON [5] Connected with Haverfordwest by a road lined with trim villas, flowering trees and wrought-iron gates. The village nucleus is small. View from the church porch. The church largely rebuilt in 1870, but the saddle-back tower, three Perpendicular windows and a Norman font remain. Whitefriars glass in east window and a modern decorated ceiling over the chancel.

WALTON EAST [5] Rather a dreary cluster of grey detached houses in the centre of which stands the mid-Victorian, simple, bellcote church, with plenty of 20c stained glass.

WALTON WEST [5] *Little Haven* is a lobster-pot village with a sheltered beach. But it has non-holiday life of its own, which saves it. Rhododendrons are in full flower in January. The path past the Swan Inn takes you quickly to the point, and splendid views of St Bride's Bay. Nearby *Broad Haven* has a fine stretch of firm sand and considerable new building on the rising ground inland. It now has a settled, all-the-year-round community, as you can see at times when parents leave or collect their children at the village school, next to tree-shaded Hepzibah chapel, 1841, slightly back from the sea front. There is considerable local opposition to further development. The Pembrokeshire Countryside Unit has an Information building in the car park at the north-

Tenby

ern entrance to the village. As well as organising field excursions and providing reading facilities and information it maintains, outside, a weather station and information board; sample items on the latter for October 12th 1972 read "Seal pups have already been born at Pwllderi and the Deer Park (Marloes); Large migration of snipe and goldfinches; August too dry for mushrooms". John Barrett is the Director, and the centre is open from April to the end of September. All that remains of the medieval inland church is the shortened saddle-back roof at the west end—the

pp176/177 Pattern and texture: ▷
Trevine

175

Carreg Samson, **Mathry**

Gwal y Filiast, see **Llanboidy**

Index

Wizo, Fleming, *see* Wiston (P)
Wogan's Cave, *see* Pembroke (P)
Woodstock, *see* Ambleston (P)
Woollen Mills, *see* Llangeler (C), Llanybyther (C),
  Ambleston (P), Granston (P), Whitechurch (P)
Worst, W. S., architect, *see* Llanelli (C)

Wyatville, Sir F., architect, *see* Llanfihangel
  Aberbythych (C)

Youth Hostels, *see* Llanddeusant (C), Llanwnda (P)
Ystradffin Farm and Stud, *see* Llanfair a'r y bryn
  (C)